Discovering SIERRA MAMMALS

by
RUSSELL K. GRATER

Illustrated by
TOM A. BLAUE

Author and Artist

Russ Grater has been interested in the great out-of-doors his whole life. For 33 years he was associated with the National Park Service as Park Naturalist in areas such as Zion National Park, Mt. Rainier National Park, Sequoia and Kings Canyon National Parks, Yosemite National Park and also as Regional Naturalist, with responsibilities in five western states. During this period, he became intimately acquainted with the wildlife about which he writes. He is the author of "Birds of Zion, Bryce and Cedar Breaks," "The Interpreters Handbook" and co-author of "Mammals of Mount Rainier National Park."

Mr. Grater is retired and makes his home in Boulder City, Nevada.

Tom Blaue was born and raised in the Colorado Rocky Mountains. He attended the University of Colorado and now makes his home in the tiny village of Allenspark, Colorado, close to Rocky Mountain National Park. As an artist, Tom has illustrated several publications, his most recent being "Plants of Zion National Park." He is presently involved in producing a series of nature art prints which will appear in a limited edition.

Published by

Yosemite
Association

Sequoia Natural
History Association

in cooperation with the National Park Service
U.S. Department of Interior

Table
of Contents

Acknowledgments

The mammals of the Sierra have been studied in past years by several outstanding biologists, including Lowell Sumner, Joseph Dixon, Victor H. Cahalane, Dr. Harold C. Bryant, Dr. Joseph Grinnell, Dr. Tracy I. Storer, Dr. Robert T. Orr, Dr. Lloyd G. Ingles and Harold E. Basey. I have made full use of their findings in preparing this manuscript. I also obtained valuable field data from members of my staff while I was Chief Park Naturalist at Sequoia and Kings Canyon National Parks, and from Douglass Hubbard and Harry Parker, formerly of the naturalist staff at Yosemite National Park.

I also wish to express my special appreciation to John Palmer, Chief Park Naturalist of Sequoia and Kings Canyon National Parks, and to Henry Berrey of the Yosemite Natural History Association under whose helpful guidance this manuscript was prepared.

Introduction

In our national parks you have the chance to see and study wild animals in a natural setting. There is nothing to keep them from roaming where they choose, and their instinctive wariness of man is greatly reduced. The parks are great sanctuaries, and most creatures of the wild quickly sense the protection such areas afford, and are thus more readily observed.

In the parks, there is little conflict between man and animal. The wild creatures' lives are relatively undisturbed by man's presence. It is in such a setting and atmosphere that you have the opportunity to see the animals living under natural conditions.

This is the animals' world and you are here as a visitor. Explore and enjoy their wilderness home, but please leave it and them none the worse for your visit.

Wildlife
History
in the
Parks

"The more things change, the more they stay the same." This is certainly true of the wildlife in Yosemite and Sequoia–Kings Canyon National Parks. Over the years some changes have occurred in the wildlife scene, yet today there is little to indicate the animal populations are appreciably different from what they were when the first white explorers entered the Sierra. From their written accounts, it is clear that the animals you see today in the meadows and forests, around the lakes and streams, are much the same as when those observations were made. But not exactly the same ones. Over the intervening years the resident wildlife have experienced a number of drastic changes.

The greatest loss to Sierran wildlife was undoubtedly the extermination of the California grizzly—also known as the "golden bear." This great carnivore once roamed the mountains and valleys from the Sierra to the Coast Range and up to the forested regions as high as 8500 feet. During the Spanish occupation of California, it was great sport for the *vaqueros*—the Spanish cowboys—to lasso the great beast before killing it. Captured grizzlies were pitted against bulls—a much publicized sporting event. With the advent of the high-powered rifle, the grizzly's doom was sealed. The last one known to have dwelt in the Sierra was reported from Sequoia National Park in 1922. The bear on the state flag of California is a mute memorial to this great animal. No single species has filled the grizzly's niche in nature. Instead several animals now occupy much of its place in the environment.

Reports of wolves having been sighted in this part of the Sierra are only reports. There have been no authenticated records of wolves in California, except for three animals taken near the Nevada boundary during the period from 1922–24. A somewhat mangy looking wolf was killed on March 22, 1962 in the foothills several miles west of Sequoia National Park, but it was determined to have been one that had escaped from captivity. Visitors in Sequoia reported seeing a wolf along a park road on March 28, 1962 and again on August 4, 1962. Sight records are difficult to verify and it is believed that the animals seen were large coyotes. Lacking proof, it seems safe to say that wolves have not been a part of the native animal life of these three parks within historic time.

Bighorn once roamed much, if not all, of the High Sierra, prior to the arrival of white settlers. They were almost exterminated in the late 1800's when domestic sheep were brought in to graze the highlands. The sheep carried diseases fatal to the bighorn, and also competed with them for the sparse feed. The rifle also played a major role in the rapid decimation of the big horn population. By 1900, there were none of these magnificent animals left in or near Yosemite, and only small bands ranged into Sequoia and Kings Canyon from their homes on the east side of the Sierran crest. A gradual recovery is now taking place, with bighorn slowly spreading back into their old territory. Given protection it is believed these animals will one day be a familiar sight among the granite crags and peaks in the three parks.

Tule elk were once common in the San Joaquin Valley, but the settling of the valley in the late 1800's reduced their numbers at an alarming rate. Hoping to preserve this fine species, a herd of twenty animals was placed in a fenced enclosure in Sequoia National Park in 1904–05. The fence burned in 1910 and the elk disappeared into the surrounding forest. The last one ever seen in Sequoia was reported in 1926. In the meantime, a twenty-eight-acre area was fenced on the floor of Yosemite Valley and a herd of ten elk was put there in 1921. In 1933, this herd, now increased to twenty-seven animals, was moved to a reserve in the Owens Valley of California. It is now considerably larger and may be seen there still.

Its impact is yet to be evaluated, but the invasion of the opossum into the parks may pose a threat to the native wildlife because of its adaptability and success in competing for food. Two other non-native mammals, the familiar house mouse and the obnoxious roof rat, have been reported in Yosemite Valley. Neither has been seen in recent years, and it is hoped that they have been exterminated. Domestic cats, probably abandoned by park visitors, are seen occasionally, but most do not survive for long.

In spite of these changes, the mammal populations in the three parks have remained relatively stable. Nature tends to balance conditions when disturbances occur.

Park Wildlife and Man

Animals in the national parks may seem tame because they are protected from man and so have not learned to fear this two-legged predator. Deer wander through the campgrounds and around parking areas along the roads. Chipmunks and ground squirrels are commonly observed. Bears grow bold and sometimes become aggressive in their search for food. The camper's food box too often becomes the object of a visit!

All parks are wildlife refuges, and every effort is made to give the animals as natural an environment as possible. They are expected to live off of the land, obtaining their food as nature intended. "Human food" is harmful to their health, and park visitors are urged not to feed them. Too often the warning goes unheeded.

As an example, a mother deer was observed begging for handouts at one of the parking areas. By actual count she was seen to eat thirteen pieces of candy—plus an assortment of cookies, bread and stale cake! Picture what effect this had on the digestive machinery of an animal designed to eat grass and browse plants—and on the quality of the milk her fawns were getting!

Feeding peanuts to chipmunks and ground squirrels is lots of fun for the kiddies. Of itself, peanuts may not be particularly harmful, but the practice encourages large numbers of these creatures to collect where visitors can feed them. This can prove to be disastrous. There is always the possibility that one of the animals doing the begging may be diseased, and thus may infect all the others with whom it comes in contact.

As for the bear, he often starts down the path to destruction when still a cub. During his first summer, his mother may visit a campground to see what goodies the garbage cans contain. Here the cub may meet an admiring but thoughtless camper and soon learns what candy bars are all about! The summer passes and the cub grows fat on all the tasty things he has been fed. Then he goes into his winter sleep. In the spring, he emerges from his winter den and sets out to find the sources of all the good things he got so easily last year. And there they are! When he hurries up to get his handout things may not happen as he expects. He is no longer a cute little cub. He is now a young bear weighing as much as forty pounds or more, and he may appear somewhat menacing to the visitor. This time he may get a cookie, or he may be yelled at or stoned. This reversal must be confusing to the bear, but he soon learns that when a hand is held out, it means food, but that when the hand is drawn back, he had better run. So he ends the summer a wiser bear but still craving handouts. The story is repeated the next spring, but now almost grown the bear searches for new ways to get food. Soon he graduates to raiding garbage cans. It is only a short step now to robbing a camper's food box. The bear is now a potential danger to people, and too often it is only a matter of time before he must be destroyed.

So we can ask ourselves, "Who killed the bear? Was it a ranger—or was it the visitors who started feeding the cub?"

Enjoy the animals, but please resist the impulse to feed them.

Unlike some refuges, hunting is not allowed in the national parks. All the animals in the park are a part of the natural scene, even those that are sometimes considered to be destructive elsewhere. However, situations may arise when wildlife management is occasionally necessary; certain species of animal must be reduced in number. For example, there have been times when the deer population in these parks increased too rapidly for the amount of food available, and the animals began to destroy the vegetative cover. Lacking sufficient numbers of predators such as cougars, bobcats and coyotes, the deer population zoomed upward. There was only one answer to the problem; the deer population had to be reduced in selected areas. This was accomplished by live-trapping deer and releasing them in less populated regions or by the selective shooting of a prescribed number. Sometimes wildlife management is essential to insure the welfare of the animals and the park.

Some park animals are so scarce that they are considered to be in danger of extinction. Only rigid protection gives them a chance to survive. Such park animals as the wolverine, fisher and bighorn—all listed as threatened species in the Sierra Nevada—are present and believed to be maintaining normal populations.

The vast forests, mountains, lakes and valleys of these three parks are the homes of more than seventy-five kinds of mammals. Man is only a visitor. If we, the visitors, relate to the animals as we should, they will continue to thrive in their wilderness surroundings. Observe, enjoy, appreciate them, but do not disturb them.

Sierran Habitats

The Sierra Nevada offers a wide variety of climates, elevations, and habitats. It stretches 350 miles (560km) in a general north to south direction and is some 60 to 80 miles (90km –130km) wide. Its western borders are 1,500 feet (461m) above sea level, but its highest peaks top 14,000 feet (4308m).

In the rolling foothills, the summers are hot and dry, the winters moist and cool. In the higher elevations, where the meadows are lush and many lakes hang in glacier-carved basins, summers are cool and moist; winters are cold, with early and heavy snowfalls. Between these extremes lies a broad climatic zone where magnificent forests and green meadows flourish and numerous streams tumble. Here the climate is relatively mild both summer and winter. With such a range of climate, plants and animals have become established, each in the habitat to which it was best able to adapt.

The lowlands, extending from near sea level to around 4,000 feet (1,200m), reach into Sequoia and Yosemite National Parks. Here the small mammals are active throughout the year and seldom venture from their established territories. However, during the fall and winter months, some mammals from the higher elevations drift down into the lowlands to escape the winter snows and seek more abundant food. Deer, bears, and gray squirrels are frequently seen migrating from the higher elevation into this land of digger pine, blue oak, buckbrush, manzanita, and chamise.

The middle elevations range from 4,000 to 7,000 feet (1,200 to 2,100m). They are characterized by forests of ponderosa pine, white fir, Douglas fir, sugar pine, and giant sequoia. Here the small mammals stay close to their home territories. The larger species, such as deer, bear, coyote, bobcat, and cougar may move into the highlands during the summer seeking better food sources, but some remain in the middle elevations where plant and animal food is usually plentiful. Most of the animals in this region are active throughout the year. A few, such as the chipmunk and bear, may sleep most of the winter.

The highlands are 7,000 feet to 14,000 feet (2,100 to 4,300m) in elevation. Here some of the small mammals hibernate during the winter, but are menaced by an influx of predators from the middle elevations in the summer. The marmot and the ground squirrel are in this group. Others, such as the pika and the jackrabbit, adapt to winter conditions and remain active. Two of the larger predators, the wolverine and fisher, roam the highlands throughout the year, occasionally dropping down into the middle elevations.

Plants and animals commonly found together in these various elevational and climatic zones constitute what is termed an "ecosystem." Thus, once it is established what type of plant cover exists in a given area, you can easily predict what mammals and other forms of wildlife are likely to be found there.

Getting to Know Park Animals

Trying to see or study animals in the wilds is generally difficult and always tedious. Most fail to appear when you want to see them, or appear and quickly disappear, allowing little time for observation. However, learning to observe them is the first step toward enjoying them.

To begin your studies, start with the animals that frequent the campgrounds or other areas of visitor interest. The animals you are most likely to see will include chipmunks, ground squirrels, and possibly deer. Watch closely to see how they behave and where they go.

Try strolling down a forest trail, or walk along the edge of a meadow. Avoid groups of people, as most animals are easily frightened. Consider the color of your clothing and don't wear white, it makes you too conspicuous. Darker shades are better. Walk slowly. When you see an animal, don't make quick movements. If you should come upon one, such as a deer or a squirrel, continue slowly so as not to alarm it. Stop to watch it when you are still some distance away. If you want to see an animal that has disappeared into a burrow—a marmot, ground squirrel or a mouse—find a comfortable place to sit and remain quiet. Usually it will reappear in a short time to see where you are and what you are doing. Watch for evidences of mammal activities, such as dens, trails in the grass, or piles of "kitchen middens" where squirrels have cut away the scales of pine cones. Watch, too, for holes dug where pine nuts or acorns have been buried. Be alert to tracks on the trail. These are most noticeable in the early morning, before hikers' feet have stirred up the dirt and destroyed them.

As your studies continue, you will find that every animal is a part of a process called a "food chain." To learn how any mammal fits into a wilderness ecosystem you will need to know what part of the chain it occupies. There are hundreds of such chains, but they all function in the same way. Simply stated, the food chain is a process whereby energy from the sun is stored by plants or animals. Plants gather the sun's energy in their growth processes and store it as food in their leaves, buds, and other growing tissues. The plant is called a food "producer." When an animal eats any part of the plant, it receives the stored energy. This animal becomes a "primary food consumer." When the animal is eaten, the energy (in reduced quantity) is acquired by the predator that ate it. This predator is called a "secondary food consumer." This process continues until there is no predator capable of killing and eating the last possessor of the now much-reduced energy. The top of the food chain has been reached. The death of the animal at the top of the chain returns this energy to lesser life forms. Part of the dead animal may furnish a meal for a carrion eater, some may be consumed by fly larvae, while the rest of the animal will return to the soil, where it will be processed by bacteria and fungi into soil nutrients for plant life to utilize. Thus the process begins again. There are food chains within food chains, usually of great complexity.

Most mammals, including man, are territorial. We build fences around our property to announce that it is ours. Animals in the wild claim an area that provides sufficient food, water, and cover to meet their needs. They may mark their territories in some way to warn others of their kind to stay out. Urine is often used for this purpose. Some of these territories are necessarily large, as in the case of cougars; others may include only a few square yards, as in the case of the meadow mouse. Animals defend their territories against encroachment by newcomers. This makes it difficult for young animals first away from home to become established.

The larger predators, such as the bear, cougar, bobcat, coyote, fox and raccoon are generally of greatest interest to the park visitor. In a way this is unfortunate, as we tend to lose sight of the smaller species that make it possible for the larger ones to survive. Without the food source provided by the vast populations of mice, woodrats, pocket gophers, squirrels, birds, and even reptiles, the larger predators would cease to exist.

If you really want to learn about mammals, you need to know something about the relationships that exist between them and their neighbors in the wildlife community.

How to Use
This Book

Each species description in this book tells you how that animal lives and some of the problems it encounters. The section titled OCCURRENCE AND DISTRIBUTION gives the relative abundance of the animal and tells in what part of the Sierra it is found. The following terms are used:

Abundant: Easily found in its preferred habitat, even by an inexperienced observer.

Common: Usually found in its preferred habitat by an average observer.

Uncommon: Difficult to find in its preferred habitat, even by an experienced observer.

Rare: Seldom observed; three or fewer confirmed sightings a year.

Foothill Zone: Elevations from approximately 1,500 to 4,000 feet (450m–1,200m). Digger pine, live and blue oaks, chaparral.

Mid-Sierra Zone: Elevations from approximately 4,000 to 7,000 feet (1,200m–2,100m). Ponderosa pine, white fir, incense cedar, California black oak, sugar pine, giant sequoia.

High Sierra Zone: Elevations from approximately 7,000 to 14,000 feet (2,100m–4,300m). Lodgepole pine, red fir, white pine, limber pine, mountain hemlock, Sierra juniper.

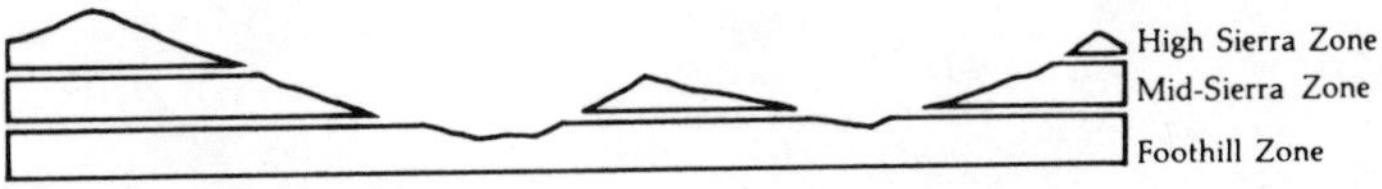

High Sierra Zone
Mid-Sierra Zone
Foothill Zone

The Hoofed Animals

Two Sierran mammals form this group, the mule deer, commonly seen in many areas, and the bighorn or mountain sheep, found only in remote, undisturbed areas.

Each is next to the top of the food chain, thus are prey for only the largest predators, one of which is man.

Mule Deer

Odocoileus hemionus

The mule deer is probably the most familiar of the Sierran mammals. The park visitor often regards it as a gentle, harmless, semidomesticated animal—a sort of true-life Bambi. Deer, especially fawns, are appealing, and there is frequently a strong urge to pet them and offer them something to eat. You may be disconcerted to find that, while the fawn seems to live up to its image, the mature deer will show irritation at being petted or by having food withheld, and will sometimes attack you with flailing front hooves. If it is a male deer, with fully developed antlers, the consequences can be quite serious. For your own safety—or your child's —don't try to get close to any animal. Admire it from a distance and above all, never attempt to feed it.

Seeing a wild deer is a greater thrill than meeting one begging in a parking lot or standing along the roadside looking expectant. It is seldom found in dense forests. More often it is seen in the early morning and late evening around small meadows and on brushy slopes. Its day is usually spent resting among tall meadow grasses or in a shallow, scraped-out hollow beneath a protective shrub or tree. Its main source of food is in the meadows or around the borders, and it seldom moves very far away.

Deer eat a wide variety of foods and seldom go hungry during the spring and summer months. Their diet is primarily the leaves and twigs of deerbush, elderberry, manzanita, thimbleberry, bittercherry, gooseberry, currant, aspen, willow, and oak. Some tender grass is eaten in the spring. They are also fond of mushrooms. In the fall, they eat acorns. In the winter months, when snow covers the middle and high elevations, they move to the snow-free lowlands where their diet may include the foliage of various evergreens.

Fall is an active season for deer. They must prepare themselves physically for the cold months that will soon arrive. It is also the time when mating takes place. In October or November, each buck tries to round up one or more does with whom he will then mate. Fights between competing bucks become common, although these encounters are more of a shoving contest than a bloody battle. There have been occasions, however, where the antlers of the two deer become locked together and they are unable to free themselves. When this happens they either die of starvation or are killed by some predator.

By December or early January, the mating season is over and the herd will have moved into the area it will occupy for the rest of the winter. Food and safety are now its main concerns. By late winter the bucks have shed their antlers. In such a herd, the bucks are difficult to distinguish from the does.

In late spring the deer move upward as the snows melt, and by late June or early July they will have reached their summer range. Now each doe must select a place to bear her young. Usually she will give birth to two fawns, although sometimes she may have one or three. Great care is taken in selecting a place where she can hide them from danger. Usually this is under a bush or where the vegetation is tall enough to hide them. When first born, the fawns have spotted coats, which makes them difficult to see when lying quietly in their hiding place. Since they have not yet acquired the strong odor of an adult deer, it is difficult for predators to find them. Instinctively the fawns remain quiet, even when danger is near. If they become so frightened they flee their hiding place, they run until they find another place to hide and there curl up again and remain quiet. Fawns stay with the doe through their first winter. By spring they have lost their spots and are capable of taking care of themselves.

Some time ago, a very young fawn was hidden by its mother in the garden at the Ahwahnee Hotel in Yosemite Valley. Visitors walking through the garden disturbed it, and it dashed away in search of a new hiding place. Everywhere it went it encountered more visitors. Frantically, it ran on looking for a place to hide, its path leading straight into the hotel lobby where it scrambled under the information desk and "froze"! A ranger carefully returned it to the garden, none the worse for its scare.

Several animals prey on deer, the most successful being the cougar, or mountain lion. While it is not known how many deer are killed each year by this big cat, estimates have put it at about one deer every ten days. The majority of the kills are of old, diseased, or careless animals. Thus, the cougar helps keep the deer population at an acceptable level by weeding out the unfit. Coyotes and bobcats also kill deer, especially when they come upon one caught in deep snow. Bears will occasionally find and eat a fawn. Some are killed each year on the park roads by cars, most of these occurring at night. In spite of these drains on the population, the deer continues to be the most abundant large mammal in the Sierra.

A subscpecies of the mule deer in nothern California and the Northwest is known as the "black-tail deer." It ranges into the northern part of Yosemite, but its relative abundance in the park is unknown.

OCCURRENCE AND DISTRIBUTION:

Sequoia–Kings Canyon: Abundant generally. Mid-Sierra and High Sierra Zones, entering the Foothill Zone in winter.

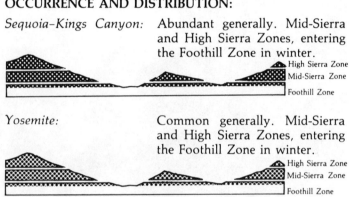

High Sierra Zone

Mid-Sierra Zone

Foothill Zone

Yosemite: Common generally. Mid-Sierra and High Sierra Zones, entering the Foothill Zone in winter.

High Sierra Zone

Mid-Sierra Zone

Foothill Zone

Bighorn

(Mountain Sheep)
Ovis canadensis

Few wilderness experiences can surpass the sight of a bighorn in its natural setting. Not only is it a magnificent animal, serene and graceful, but its home always affords an outstanding backdrop. The bighorn is a mountain dweller, and among the lofty crags and steep slopes are where it is most often observed. However, you may look a long time before you see one. In such an environment its drab coloration enables it to blend into its surroundings, making it difficult to see. Frequently, even sharp eyes aided by binoculars fail to locate the animal, and not until the bighorn moves is it noticed. It sometimes crosses small valleys as it moves from one mountainous area to another. It shuns broad, open spaces, apparently feeling insecure if it wanders far from its rugged highlands.

The bighorn appears to follow a daily routine. In the early morning it eats until it is satisfied; then it retires to a place affording a clear view of the surrounding country. There it lies and chews its cud. Like the domestic cow, it has a compartmented stomach. The food it consumes while grazing enters the first stomach where it remains until the animal is at rest. Ball-like "cuds" are then returned to the mouth to be rechewed. The thoroughly ground-up food then goes to the other stomach divisions to be digested. In early afternoon the bighorn may eat again; then it rests and sleeps some more. A third meal, of considerable quantity, is consumed in late afternoon, and by dusk it has retired for the night. It chooses its sleeping site carefully, usually a place under the crest of a ridge where stalking predators would find it difficult to approach without being heard.

The bighorn is a sociable animal and several usually range together. Each band has its own home territory. This may be large or small, depending on how much food and water is available.

The bighorn's principal food is grass, but it also eats buds of browse plants, such as aspen and willow. If necessary, it can go without water for several days at a time, since the plants it eats contain enough moisture to supply part of its requirements.

During the summer months, the rams live apart from the ewes and yearlings. Usually rams band together, but occasionally old rams seem to prefer to live alone. Late in the fall, the rams become quarrelsome as the mating season approaches. Some try to collect several ewes into a harem; others may not even bother. Spectacular fights may develop between two competing males. They approach each other, snorting, grunting, and striking out with their sharp front hooves. As though at a given signal, they move several feet apart, then suddenly wheel and charge. The sound as the two animals meet head-on can be heard for half a mile. Dazed for a few moments, they get to their feet and charge again. This may go on for as much as an hour or two with no apparent damage to either party before they decide to end the conflict. Sometimes other rams join in the fight, which then turns into a free-for-all!

Six months after mating has taken place, the lambs are born about the first week of May. One is the usual number. On rare occasions the ewe may deliver twins. In preparation for the event, she leaves the rest of the band and goes off alone to find a safe nursery. She chooses a ledge or a place in the shelter of a cliff where she can detect the approach of an enemy. Here she remains until her lamb is born. At birth, the lamb is wobbly on its feet and nearly helpless. This is a critical period in its life, for if danger threatens, the lamb can neither run nor hide. Even after it gains enough strength to get about, it remains near its birthplace for several days. During this time the mother remains on guard, leaving her lamb only long enough to obtain food and water. Soon the lamb is able to follow her on her search for food. Before long, they may band together with several other ewes and lambs.

Bighorn, especially the lambs, are subject to attack by cougar, coyote, and occasionally bobcat and wolverine. However, losses are not heavy. These predators cannot move among the cliffs and ledges as nimbly as the bighorn, and the success rate is low. Outside the national parks, the bighorn's most dangerous enemy is man with his high-powered rifle. Fortunately, these magnificent animals are protected in the Sierra. Here they seem to be holding their own, although they are still listed as a threatened species.

Most bighorn are found in the High Sierra on the east side of the Sierran crest, opposite Sequoia and Kings Canyon. They enter those parks during the spring and summer months, and then move to the eastern slope in the fall and winter. They are few in number over their entire range. They were found in the Yosemite high country prior to 1900; then none were reported until recently, although rams horns were found in some areas indicating the animal's presence. One dead ram was found in 1933, lodged in the ice at the terminus of the Lyell Glacier. Apparently it had fallen into a crevasse in the ice many years before.

OCCURRENCE AND DISTRIBUTION:

Sequoia–Kings Canyon: Rare. High Sierra Zone in summer.

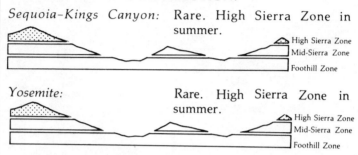

Yosemite: Rare. High Sierra Zone in summer.

The Rodents

This group comprises the most abundant species in the parks. They are primary food consumers; that is, they convert sun energy from plants into meat. This meat then serves as food for predators. All rodents are near the bottom of the food chain. Most rodents have a short life expectancy and quickly become food for a hungry hunter. However they multiply rapidly, and quickly replace numbers lost in this fashion. Some rodents are themselves predatory, eating large numbers of insects and other invertebrates. Most are present in large numbers. However, many are small, shy, and often nocturnal, and you may have to make an extra effort to see them.

Mountain Beaver

Aplodontia rufa

This stout, compact animal looks something like a tail-less muskrat. It has been given a wide assortment of names, none of which accurately describes the animal or its actions. In parts of the Northwest it is called the "boomer," but it does not boom! It is called the "whistler," but it doesn't whistle. It is also called the "sewellel," an Indian name given the animal by the white man. A sewellel is a fur robe, but may or may not be made from mountain beaver pelts. To complete the confusion, the "mountain beaver" is not a beaver. Nor is it related to one except insofar as they both are rodents.

Few people have seen a mountain beaver, and its presence in an area may not be suspected. Only sharp eyes will catch a glimpse of it or even locate its home or runways. It is primarily nocturnal although it may be active during the day. During the day it displays definite periods of activity, broken by sleep or rest. When it is awake and active, it spends most of its time foraging for food, or constructing tunnels around its home. It eats nothing but leafy plants. It prefers grass, various herbs, willow, alder, elderberry, currant, gooseberry, thimbleberry and fern, all of which are available during the summer. As fall approaches, the mountain beaver cuts large quantities of plants into manageable, short lengths, and stores them inside its burrow. This will be its winter food supply. Because the burrow is usually damp, much of this food will spoil. With the coming of winter, it adds incense cedar and fir twigs to its diet. These are obtained by climbing into the low branches of small trees.

The mountain beaver is found in moist, even wet, areas. It swims readily, but shows no preference for water. It seems to choose this wet living situation because it needs to be near drinking water; many of its numerous tunnels lead directly to a nearby stream. This vast maze of tunnels has no apparent pattern but crosses and recrosses in aimless fashion. The animal seems to dig tunnels only to get where food and water are easily obtained. It frequently digs tunnels up through the snow to reach food on the surface. Often it packs the dirt removed by underground digging into the snow tunnels, leaving evidence of the past winter's activities when the snow melts in the spring.

Several mountain beaver are usually found living together as a colony. Though the network of tunnels is apparently used by any individual, there is no evidence that sleeping quarters are shared. Little is known about their family life. Mating takes place in February or March, and the young, usually only two or three, are born about four weeks later. At birth, they are naked, blind, and completely helpless. For the first ten days they are unable to see. However, they develop rapidly after that, and by the time they are three months old, they are ready to leave the nest chamber and establish their own homes.

With a low annual birth rate, the mountain beaver would seem to be in danger of extermination. However, its choice of habitat gives protection from its enemies. It seldom moves far from a stream whose small drainages are often filled with dense growths of tangled vegetation. Such a living situation offers an abundance of food throughout most of the year, while affording shelter against preying hawks and owls. Fallen logs and brush offer added protection against coyote, fox, skunk, bobcat, and cougar, all of which find it difficult to stalk the mountain beaver outside of its burrow. The most successful predators are the weasel and mink, which can pursue it into its burrow even through the most intricate network of tunnels.

The mountain beaver's place in the ecological structure is difficult to determine. It is neither an important food source for predators, nor is it destructive to plant species. One biologist states that "the mountain beaver appears to have no object in life except to dig holes and eat. He is neither useful nor ornamental, and the sole purpose of his creation appears to be to furnish a rare and queer animal for curious naturalists to study." This biologist overlooks one important detail. The mountain beaver is one of nature's most interesting animals, and, as such, it occupies a special place in the wildlife community. We would be the poorer without it.

OCCURRENCE AND DISTRIBUTION:

Sequoia–Kings Canyon: Uncommon. Mid-Sierra Zone.

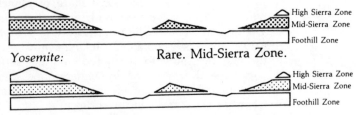

Yosemite: Rare. Mid-Sierra Zone.

Yellow-Bellied Marmot

(Whistler, Rockchuck)
Marmota flaviventris

The marmot is as much a part of the High Sierra as the jumbled rock piles where it makes its home and nearby flower-laden meadows where it obtains its food. It is as much a vital part of the highland fauna as its neighbors, the pika and the rosy finch. While it may venture into the middle elevations, its real home is in and around forest line. Any hiker into a back-country meadow can be sure he will be greeted with a short, loud, piercing whistle as a marmot sends out a warning to other marmots that an intruder is approaching. Immediately, the warning can be heard repeated around the area, as marmots, near and far, come to attention or scurry for cover. Nor does the alarm go unheeded by other animals within hearing distance. At the sound of the marmot's whistle the entire high country community becomes alert and prepares for trouble.

The marmot prefers to make its home in a broken rock slide, but it may locate under a ledge, if there are wide, protective crevices leading back into the cliff. Occasionally it will dig a burrow in the edge of a meadow, preferably where a rock will help protect the entrance. However, such a den is vulnerable to bears, wolverines, and badgers, all of which can easily dig out the marmot. A marmot that lives a reasonably long life is almost always a rock-dweller, for its enemies are numerous. Coyotes, foxes, bobcats, cougars, and eagles prey on it constantly. Only an alert marmot lives for long.

The marmot is the largest member of the squirrel family, but it neither climbs trees nor has the living habits of that family. Appearing to savor the pleasures of life, it likes to eat, grow fat and enjoy the sunshine. In the early morning and the late afternoon, it leaves its den to search for food, especially for herbs of all kinds. Summer flowers are plentiful where it lives, and are easily reached in comparative safety. It eats until its stomach bulges, then climbs a rock near the entrance to its den and basks in the warmth of the sun. Being a true sun lover, it stays inside its rocky home when the weather is cloudy. Its seemingly endless consumption of food during the summer months puts on enough fat

to see it through the winter. Instinct warns the marmot that shortly several months will arrive when there will be no food available, and it must survive on its accumulated fat. In late summer or early autumn, the marmot retires to its den to prepare for a long period of hibernation. Curled up in a grass-lined bed, it puts its front feet over its eyes and falls into a deep sleep and does not awaken until the following spring. The metabolism rate drops until the animal appears almost dead, and it can be rolled on the ground with no noticeable response. When it awakens in the spring, its fat is gone. Snow may still be on the ground, forcing it to go without food until the snow melts and green plants become available. When that happens, the marmot greedily makes up for lost time.

At the end of the hibernation period in late March or early April, the marmot sets about finding a mate. The young are born in May. Usually there are four or five babies, although as many as eight have been found in some litters. Young marmots grow very rapidly. By the time they are two months old, they have matured sufficiently to care for themselves. In a few more weeks they have reached adulthood and are already starting to prepare for the coming winter, and before fall arrives, the mother has sent them out to find their own hibernating den while she prepares hers. Most young marmots do not mate until their second year. Many fail to escape their enemies that long.

While marmot populations may vary somewhat from year to year, predators tend to keep their numbers fairly stable. Unless hit by disease or some natural catastrophe, their numbers remain remarkably high.

OCCURRENCE AND DISTRIBUTION:

Sequoia–Kings Canyon: Abundant locally. High Sierra Zone, down to about 7,000 feet (2,100m).

Yosemite: Common locally. High Sierra Zone.

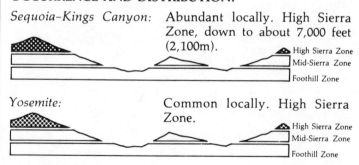

California Ground Squirrel

Spermophilus beecheyi

This animal resembles the familiar gray squirrel of the pine forests, except that it lacks the big, plumed tail. Unlike its tree-dwelling cousin, the ground squirrel prefers the dry, partially open slopes of the lowland oak forests, where it is often found living in large colonies.

The ground squirrel digs its burrow in porous soil, usually choosing a place where rocks help to protect against predators. A vast system of inter-connecting tunnels with numerous entrances is developed, allowing members of the colony to move about in relative safety. Within this network of tunnels, the animals enlarge some areas for sleeping rooms, and others for food storage. No one knows whether each squirrel reserves certain portions of this system of tunnels for its own use, or whether the tunnels are shared by all the animals in a colony. In some instances other kinds of animals may use parts of the squirrel den. Snakes, rabbits, toads, and even skunks often move in and claim "squatters rights."

In the spring the squirrel eats large quantities of green vegetation, but when summer arrives its diet changes to include several kinds of seeds, including manzanita. In the late summer and early fall, it harvests many acorns, some of which are eaten where found while others are put into storage for future use. A quail's nest may provide a two-course meal, for the squirrel eats not only the eggs but any young birds that may be present. Meat of almost any kind is eaten and animals killed along the road are frequent additions to the diet.

Baby ground squirrels arrive in late spring or early summer. The normal litter is six or seven young. The babies are born in an enlarged, usually grass-lined room in one of the tunnels. After a very brief growing-up period, the young are ready to take care of themselves. It is not known whether they leave the general area occupied by the colony.

Ground squirrels are an important link in the food chain, and make up part of the diet of foxes, bobcats, coyotes, weasels, and birds of prey. They also furnish meals for such reptiles as the kingsnake and gopher snake. Although large numbers are killed each year, the population does not fluctuate very much.

Depending upon the climate and elevation, the ground squirrel may either hibernate or aestivate. If the animal lives where snow lies on the ground throughout the winter, it hibernates, passing the winter in a dormant state. If it lives in an area where summer temperatures range too high for comfort, it may simply retire to its den and aestivate, that is remain awake but torpid awaiting cooler weather.

This squirrel is most abundant in the low valleys and foothills of the Sierra, but it is occasionally found in the highlands where terrain and ground cover are favorable. It is frequently seen along the approach roads leading into the parks. It is particularly abundant between Ash Mountain and Giant Forest in Sequoia, and between El Portal and Yosemite Valley and at the parking area of the Wawona Tunnel in Yosemite. At one time it is believed the animal was restricted to the foothills and low valleys of the Sierra. The construction of roads through the forests and the opening of large areas through logging and farming created entire new habitats, and has enabled the squirrel to spread rapidly into parts of the Sierra where it was not originally a resident species. In recent years, it has been reported as high as the 10,000-foot level in Sequoia. What effect its invasion will have upon the ecology of the middle elevations is problematical, but it is a fast-breeding and aggressive animal. Its impact upon other resident members of the squirrel family, and upon the predator population, could be pronounced.

OCCURRENCE AND DISTRIBUTION:

Sequoia–Kings Canyon: Abundant generally. Foothill Zone, spreading up to as much as 10,000 feet (3,000m).

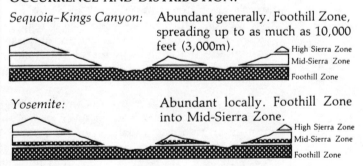

High Sierra Zone
Mid-Sierra Zone
Foothill Zone

Yosemite: Abundant locally. Foothill Zone into Mid-Sierra Zone.

High Sierra Zone
Mid-Sierra Zone
Foothill Zone

Belding
Ground
Squirrel

Spermophilus beldingi

This ground squirrel is often known as the "picket-pin,"
a name that aptly describes the way it appears when disturbed. Like its neighbor, the marmot, it utters a sharp
whistle when an intruder appears. It sits upright, looking
very much like a small stake driven into the ground, its short
tail twitching nervously as it waits to see what the intruder is
up to. It remains virtually motionless until the danger draws
alarmingly near, then it dives into its den.

The picket-pin is at home in the meadows and grasslands of the high country, and seldom leaves the open areas.
Food is obtained near the burrow, and the squirrel rarely
ventures far from the entrance. Grasses and other herbs are
its principal diet, and the meadows and slopes supply these
in abundance during the summer months. Because the warm,
growing season is short at high elevations, it eats at every
opportunity, and by the end of the summer it is nearly too
fat to run. This endless consumption of food is a necessary
preparation for the winter months ahead. In late summer or
early fall, it retires to its nest where it hibernates until the following spring. The accumulated fat on the body is slowly ab-
sorbed during this time of inactivity, and the animal becomes
quite thin. Snow may still be on the ground when the picket-
pin emerges, and new plant growth may not be available.
Fasting may have to continue until new plant growth appears. This is a situation that the squirrel apparently handles
without difficulty. Once vegetation becomes available again,
the fat lost during the winter is quickly restored.

The squirrel chooses ground that is fairly flat and sandy
for its den. The burrow is relatively shallow, which makes the
squirrel susceptible to attack from predators adept at digging.
The coyote, for example, is a constant menace, and is often
successful in digging out the occupant of the den. However,
among the predators the badger and weasel are its most feared
enemies. With its long claws and powerful legs the badger is
able to dig the squirrel from its burrow without difficulty.
Only agility and several convenient exits from the burrow offer the squirrel a chance to escape. Even these are little protec-

tion when a weasel chooses the squirrel for a meal. Although the weasel does not dig, it can follow the picket-pin anywhere, and it keeps up a relentless pursuit of the panic-stricken animal. The chase usually ends with the weasel clamping its sharp teeth into its helpless prey. Fishers, bobcats, foxes and hawks also take their toll of the squirrel population.

Like other small animals with many predators, the ground squirrel raises large numbers of young. Mating takes place in early spring; the young begin to appear in April or early May. They number about eight or more per litter. Although helpless at birth, only a few days pass before they are ready to venture outside the den to eat green vegetation. By late summer, they are fully grown, and have spread over the area and dug their own dens. Mortality during this period is high, and the less alert individuals soon fall prey to enemies. Thus, by the time the animals are ready to hibernate, the ground squirrel population in the area is about the same as it was the previous fall.

OCCURRENCE AND DISTRIBUTION:

Sequoia–Kings Canyon: No records in southern region. Common in high meadows, High Sierra Zone in north.

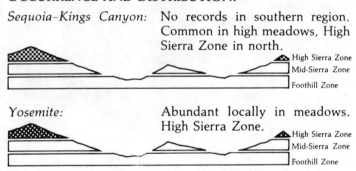

Yosemite: Abundant locally in meadows. High Sierra Zone.

Golden-Mantled Ground Squirrel

Spermophilus lateralis

If one animal can be considered the favorite of the park visitors, it is surely the golden-mantled ground squirrel. It gathers in areas wherever people congregate and entertains everyone when it sits up and begs for food. Usually it gets more than it can eat, and it scampers away to bury the surplus. Then it hurries back to beg for more.

The golden mantle is known by several names. In some parts of the country, its reddish head has earned it the nickname of "copperhead." It is also called the "big chipmunk." This is understandable, as its striped sides resemble those of a chipmunk. However the golden mantle's stripes stop at the shoulders, while those of a chipmunk continue to its nose. Its movements are also unlike those of the chipmunk, in that it doesn't flit from place to place, but moves more leisurely.

It is an atrocious housekeeper, and its den is usually very untidy. Refuse is often scattered inside, attracting all sorts of small insects, mites and fleas. Not all the fleas stay in the den, and the squirrel does a lot of scratching to try and rid itself of the pests. It takes numerous dust baths, rolling in the dirt and fluffing up its fur so that the fine dust will get next to the skin and cause the fleas much miscomfort. Dust baths are especially effective for this purpose when taken near the base of a sequoia. The dust around the tree is made up in large part of powdered sequoia bark. This powder is high in tannic acid, which permeates the flea's breathing apparatus. In spite of its fleas and its messy home, the squirrel keeps itself neat and well groomed.

The golden mantle digs its burrow where the ground cover is light and the trees are scattered. It especially likes the edges of rock slides, and prefers to locate the entrance of the den among the rocks. It will settle for open ground if there is enough small plant life to conceal the opening. The entrance is larger than the tunnel itself, enabling the squirrel to dive quickly into the burrow when danger threatens. The tunnel goes down for several inches and then levels off, continuing for several feet before rising to the surface again. This is a safety exit and is usually hidden. Inside the burrow, the squirrel makes several side tunnels, none of which reach the suface. One is enlarged into a sleeping room, and here it makes a nest of bits of dry leaves, bark, grass, or other soft material. This becomes the summer bedroom, and is used in the daytime as well as at night. However, in winter, the burrow will not be deep enough to protect against the cold. And so before the cold months arrive, the squirrel adds more material to the nest. It goes into hibernation in September or October and enters into a heavy sleep, lasting until early spring.

The golden mantle raises fewer young each season than some other species, indicating that it is under less pressure from predators. Mating takes place soon after awakening from hibernation, usually in April. In June or early July, the young are born, normally five to a litter, although sometimes more. The mother squirrel has only one litter per year. By the time the young are a month old, they have been weaned and are on a plant diet. Now they are big enough to venture above ground, a very critical time because of predators. By September, the survivors are nearly full grown. During the summer they have put on as much fat as possible in preparation for their winter sleep. Also during this time they build their own dens and nests. Food is stored for use when they emerge from hiberation, for it is likely to be scarce at that time.

It is easy to observe the squirrel during the summer when it is searching for food. Most of what it finds is promptly eaten, the rest is stuffed into large cheek pouches and taken away to be stored for future use. A portion of the seeds and nuts it finds are put in small holes which it digs in the ground, and the rest in storerooms inside the burrow. The squirrel eats a wide assortment of food. Its diet includes pine nuts, fir seeds, acorns, berries, grasses, various flowers, mushrooms, insects and larvae. Occasionally it finds and eats a freshly killed chipmunk or other small animal.

The golden mantle lives at an elevation where predators are most commonly found, although it suffers less than other species. Nonetheless it lives under constant threat. Its plump body offers a fine meal for the coyote, bobcat, marten, fox and the always dreaded weasel. If it escapes these, it may fall victim to a goshawk or a Cooper's hawk, both skilled hunters of the forest. The day to day life of a golden-mantled ground squirrel is not always pleasant to contemplate. Nevertheless it continues to thrive.

OCCURRENCE AND DISTRIBUTION:

Sequoia–Kings Canyon: Abundant. Mid-Sierra Zone into High Sierra Zone.

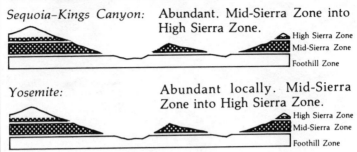

Yosemite: Abundant locally. Mid-Sierra Zone into High Sierra Zone.

Chipmunk
Eutamias (ssp.)

The chipmunk rivals the golden-mantled ground squirrel wherever visitors congregate, and for the same reason—to enjoy hand-outs of everything from peanuts to candy. Some of the tidbits are taken to the nearest shelter where they are daintily consumed. Non-perishable items, such as peanuts, may be stored in small caches in the ground or in its burrow. Then it scurries back for more. When running, it seems to barely touch the ground as it flits from the shelter of one bush or rock to another. It often stops en route for a look around for danger, poised motionless, except for the slowly waving tail. Its color pattern, aided by the narrow stripes on its back and head, serve as a camouflage giving it some protection from any enemies in the area.

Some species of chipmunks climb trees almost as readily as a tree squirrel, sometimes reaching dizzying heights. During the season for harvesting seeds, it has been observed high in the top of a huge sequoia, cutting the ripening cones. It collects and stores hundreds of pine nuts and acorns, stuffing them into its cheek pouches a few at a time and unloading them in its winter storehouse. Many are also cached away in small holes. Some of these nuts and acorns are never retrieved and sprout into seedlings. Many of the trees you see in the forest were undoubtedly planted because of the chipmunk's instinct to bury surplus seeds and nuts. Its food list is extensive, and it seems to eat anything. Currant, gooseberry, manzanita, dogwood, elderberry, and thimbleberry are high on the list. It also relishes seed-bearing plants, such as the grasses, aster, and thistle; bulbs of various kinds; mushrooms; several kinds of flowers and tender buds. Beetles, grasshoppers and caterpillars also form part of its diet.

In its choice of home sites, the chipmunk is somewhat restricted. Its front feet are so tiny that it can only dig its burrow where the soil is not hard. Loose dirt under fallen trees offers a choice place for a tunnel, especially if it can be dug back under the log; this affords protection against digging predators. Old rotten logs are favorite spots, for the decaying wood is easy to tunnel, and a nest can be made in such a location without difficulty. Deserted woodpecker holes also offer excellent sites. A chipmunk's nest is simple. Usually it is lined with shredded grass, bits of bark, or lichens. The chipmunk is a clean animal, and the condition of its home reflects its tidy habits. In spite of all its efforts to be clean, it is plagued by fleas. It takes daily dust baths to discourage the tiny pests.

Chipmunks at lower elevations are active throughout the year, but those in the snow country retire to their nests for the winter in September or October. They do not accumulate fat for the winter sleep as do the ground squirrels, for they do not hibernate in the true sense. They simply become inactive and torpid. Their winter sleep is irregular, and they frequently awake to eat some of the nuts from their food store. In late spring, depending on the weather conditions outside the den, the chipmunk emerges and mating takes place in a few days. Chipmunks in the lower elevations give birth to three to six young in May, while babies in the snow zone arrive later, usually in July. The young remain with their mother for about six weeks; then they wander away to establish their own homes. The mother may mate again and have a second litter before the summer's end.

As is true of other small rodents, the first few days of the young chipmunk's life away from its mother are critical. If it has learned to be wary, it may survive. If not, it will soon provide a meal for one of its many predators. Its most deadly enemy is the weasel, which can follow the chipmunk wherever it goes. Relentlessly it continues the chase until the catch is made. In addition, the chipmunk must be constantly on watch for hawks, foxes, and pine martens, as well as for snakes that are able to enter the den. Bears, too, are a menace, for they can rip open the chipmunk's rotten-log home without difficulty and gobble up an entire family.

Several species of chipmunks are found in the Sierran parks. Although similar in appearance, they differ somewhat in coloration, size, voice, and choice of habitat.

OCCURRENCE AND DISTRIBUTION:

Alpine Chipmunk *(Eutamias alpinus)*
Sequoia–Kings Canyon: Common. High Sierra Zone.

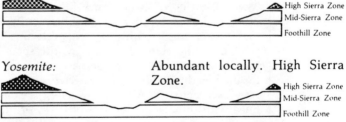

Yosemite: Abundant locally. High Sierra Zone.

Lodgepole Chipmunk *(Eutamias speciosus)*

Sequoia–Kings Canyon: Abundant. Mid-Sierra Zone into High Sierra Zone.

High Sierra Zone
Mid-Sierra Zone
Foothill Zone

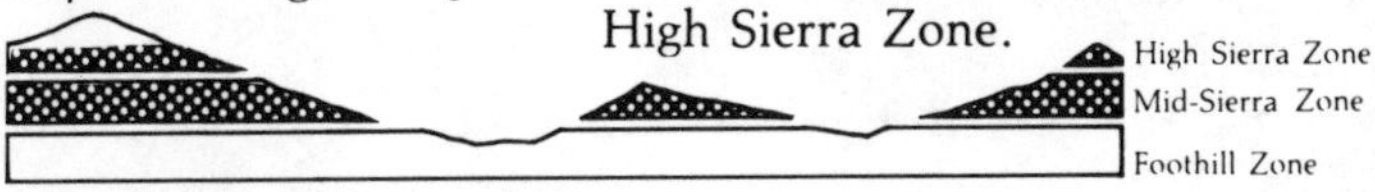

Yosemite: Abundant locally. Mid-Sierra Zone into High Sierra Zone.

High Sierra Zone
Mid-Sierra Zone
Foothill Zone

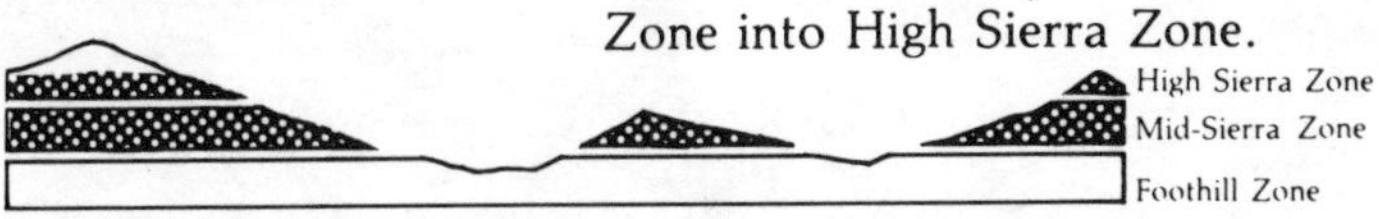

Long-eared Chipmunk *(Eutamias quadrimaculatus)*

Sequoia–Kings Canyon: Not recorded.
Yosemite: Common. Mid-Sierra Zone.

High Sierra Zone
Mid-Sierra Zone
Foothill Zone

Merriam Chipmunk *(Eutamias merriami)*

Sequoia–Kings Canyon: Uncommon. Foothill Zone.

High Sierra Zone
Mid-Sierra Zone
Foothill Zone

Yosemite: Uncommon. Foothill Zone into lower Mid-Sierra Zone.

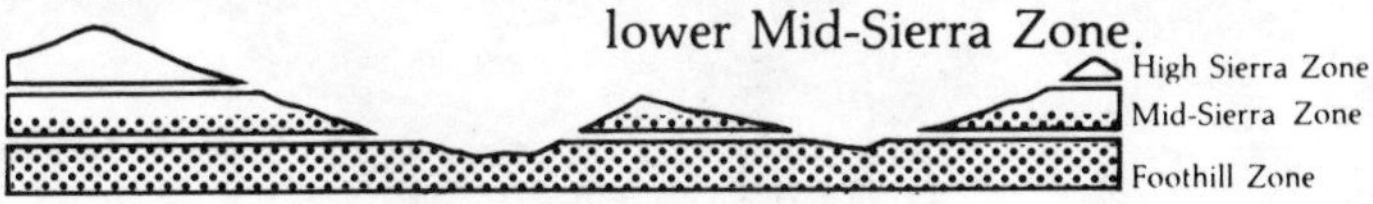

High Sierra Zone
Mid-Sierra Zone
Foothill Zone

Townsend Chipmunk *(Eutamias townsendi)*

Sequoia–Kings Canyon: Not recorded.
Yosemite: Common generally. Mid-Sierra Zone.

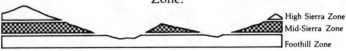

High Sierra Zone
Mid-Sierra Zone
Foothill Zone

Western Gray Squirrel

Sciurus griseus

It may seem strange, but if you want to see this squirrel, look first on the ground, not in the trees. When it is in a tree it will remain quiet, watching to see what you are going to do. Its soft, gray fur blends almost perfectly with the branches, making it difficult to see. Unlike its cousin, the chickaree, it is not a noisy animal, and does little to give away its location. It spends most of its time on the ground hunting for food, or investigating anything that looks interesting. Even there it moves slowly and is difficult to pick out against the neutral tones of dead pine needles and old vegetation. The huge plumed tail which the squirrel carries is often the first thing to be noticed. While it is not especially afraid of people, it avoids getting close to them. It is an expert at traveling in the trees. It runs among the branches with complete assurance and leaps easily from one tree to another. It is active throughout the year, and only severe weather will drive a gray squirrel to cover.

Deep snow is no problem for the gray squirrel. Thus it does not need to collect and store quantities of food for the winter. Instead, it searches out the food it needs each day. It may cut a green pine cone and chip away the scales one by one to get at the seeds. Usually it eats only what it wants at the moment; it will come back later for the rest of the cone. It sits at the base of a tree or on a nearby rock to work on cones, and a large pile of cone scales, called a "midden," accumulates where it has been eating. It eats a variety of food, but pine nuts and acorns are its favorite food. Both are available over a long harvest season. Some acorns and pine nuts may be buried and dug up again as needed. Many of these are never found again. Like the chickaree and the chipmunk, the gray squirrel is responsible for planting many oak and pine seedlings. On the other hand it doesn't hesitate to rob the acorn caches of the Acorn Woodpecker. It is also fond of mushrooms and is often seen searching for them in promising areas. It eats bird eggs and some young birds.

The gray squirrel will build its nest in a hollow limb or tree trunk, if it can find one. Living in the oak belt, old trees often provide an inviting location. It may, however, build a nest among the thick branches near the top of a tree. It first constructs a platform of sticks and leafy twigs. On top of this it places bits of bark and smaller twigs. Inside this nest, it makes a bed of soft grass. Here it will sleep and raise its young.

Mating takes place during the winter months. The male then goes his way, leaving the female to rear the young. The young are born in the spring. There are normally three or four in a litter, although there may be as few as two or as many as five. Like other tree squirrel young, they will be blind for about five weeks; after that they will develop rapidly.

The gray squirrel has many enemies. The coyote, fox, marten, weasel, bobcat, Cooper's hawk, and goshawk hunt throughout the year. The kingsnake and the rattlesnake are also threats during the summer. In spite of these hunting pressures, the gray squirrel maintains a rather steady population unless hit by disease. Epidemics in the past almost wiped out the gray squirrel populations in Yosemite Valley and near Giant Forest in Sequoia. Populations have always returned to normal in a few years.

OCCURRENCE AND DISTRIBUTION:

Sequoia–Kings Canyon: Abundant generally. Mid-Sierra Zone.

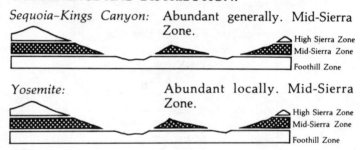

Yosemite: Abundant locally. Mid-Sierra Zone.

Chickaree

(Douglas Squirrel)
Tamiasciurus douglasii

Anyone who enters a forest in the Mid- to High Sierra Zone is almost certain to have his right to be there disputed by this vociferous bundle of energy. It bounces across the road or trail, races up a convenient tree, and, sitting on a branch or half hidden behind the tree trunk, voices its feelings of any intrusion into what it apparently feels is its own domain. The pine and fir forests are its home, and it continuously reminds all who will listen that such is true.

Known as the chickaree in the Far West, it also has other names such as "pine squirrel" and "Douglas squirrel." It is strictly a daytime animal, rising early in the morning and not retiring until dark. It is busy all day, probing curiously into first one thing and then another. It adapts quickly to the presence of people. Many a camper has seen food snatched from his table and carried into a tree by this saucy thief.

The chickaree does not hibernate, even when deep snow covers his home, nor does it put on much fat in preparation for the winter months. Instead, it stores large quantities of nonperishable foods that can be eaten as needed. Late summer and early fall is a busy time for all tree squirrels, and especially for the chickaree. Climbing into the tops of pine, fir, or sequoia trees, it cuts scores of cones; once a total of 1,242 sequoia cones were found piled at the base of one tree. During the harvest, the sound of cones plopping on the ground is familiar, and anyone who stands under a tree in which the squirrel is at work, risks being hit by a falling cone. Some cones, such as those of the Jeffrey pine are large and heavy enough to raise a good lump. After cutting the cones, the chickaree descends and gathers them into one place. The pine and fir cones are cut apart. It may eat the nuts at this point or it may store them. The sequoia cones may be stored, but only the seed scales will be eaten. Most of the stored nuts are cached in small holes dug in the ground, and are covered for safe-keeping. Later the chickaree will locate these caches by smell, not from memory. Many of the nuts are never dug up, and thus the squirrel has helped plant a new forest. Because the nuts come from the top of the tree, they are rich and strong and produce the best possible seedlings. The chickaree is another valuable forester. In addition

to cones from the evergreen forest, acorns are high on the list of foods. Seeds from grasses and several flower species, mushrooms, bird eggs when they can be found, are welcome additions to the diet.

The chickaree's home is hard to find. Usually it chooses a hollow tree or a hollow limb, and builds its nest well back inside, out of view. It may also build an outside nest of twigs, lichen, bits of bark, and anything else that might add to its comfort. The outside nest is usually built high in a tree where foliage conceals it from the ground. In areas where tree trunks are small and seldom have cavities, the outside nest is common.

Mating takes place in early spring, and the young make their appearance in May and June. The litter averages five, but may range between two and seven. At birth the young squirrels are naked and blind, but within about ten days their eyes have opened, and they are covered with fine fur. By the time the young squirrels are six weeks old they are able to venture out of the nest. By late summer or early fall they are building nests and storing food for the winter. Sometimes members of the family do not scatter but stay together all winter.

The chickaree has many enemies. Pine martens, fishers, and weasels climb trees easily so are most feared. Foxes and bobcats are always a threat on the ground and hawks also surprise and catch a few. Because it has so many predators to contend with, there is little likelihood of chickaree numbers becoming out of balance.

OCCURRENCE AND DISTRIBUTION:

Sequoia–Kings Canyon: Abundant generally. Mid-Sierra Zone into High Sierra Zone.

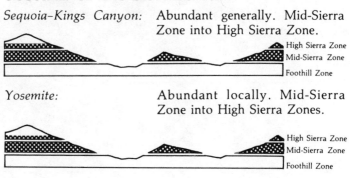

High Sierra Zone
Mid-Sierra Zone
Foothill Zone

Yosemite: Abundant locally. Mid-Sierra Zone into High Sierra Zones.

High Sierra Zone
Mid-Sierra Zone
Foothill Zone

Northern Flying Squirrel

Glaucomys sabrinus

You may never see one of these small, dark animals in the wilds. Not that the flying squirrel is rare. On the contrary, it is common in the Sierran parks. But because it is small and moves silently about only at night, its presence is difficult to detect and sightings are seldom reported. Occasionally it may reveal its whereabouts by a quick movement among the high branches or when becoming silhouetted against the sky. When it glides from one tree to another, it is possible to hear a slight thud as it lands on the tree trunk. This is followed by faint sounds as it scrambles up the tree into the higher branches.

The "flying" squirrel doesn't literally fly. Loose folds of well-furred skin stretch between the front and hind feet, giving it a "bundled up" appearance when not moving. To move between distant trees, the squirrel climbs high into the top of one and leaps into space. It spreads its four legs out wide, bringing the loose folds of skin into play. These support the squirrel as it descends rather like a glider, his flat, soft-furred tail controlling its direction. As the target is approached, it swoops upward and comes gently to rest. Then it quickly climbs higher for protection or to launch a flight to another tree.

This interesting creature may build a nest high among the branches of a tree, or it may take over and remodel one that another animal has abandoned. If it chooses the abandoned nest of a chickaree or a gray squirrel, it cleans it and adds new nesting materials. These may range from small stems, leaves, and bark, to bird feathers. If it can find where a woodpecker has hollowed out a room in an old tree branch or trunk, it moves in and takes over this choice site. An old snag is a favorite place to look for the squirrel. The nest is made only to sleep in, and it will not venture outside except at night. Often more than one squirrel occupies a nest, and they seem to get along together peacefully.

The flying squirrel appears to breed only in late winter. After about six weeks, from two to six babies are born. They weigh only about one-fifth of an ounce apiece and are naked and blind. Although their ears are sealed, certain sounds may be audible to them. About two weeks after birth, the young squirrel has a fully-furred body, but it cannot see for another two weeks. After six weeks its mother begins to add bits of tender plant buds and insects to its milk diet, and by the end of the summer it is able to take care of itself. It may find a new home in a nearby hollow tree, or it may remain with its mother and the rest of the family until she is ready to give birth to a new litter.

Lichens are this forest creature's main food. It also eats nuts, seeds, mushrooms, various fruits, berries, insects and tender tree buds. It may invade birds' nests to steal the eggs. It also likes meat and has been known to enter campgrounds and help itself to any butter, bacon, fish, or any other meat that has been left unprotected.

The flying squirrel has many enemies, but few that are successful. Occasionally a marten, weasel, fisher, or owl catches one, but other predators have little success. Because they do not experience heavy predation, flying squirrels are able to maintain a stable population throughout the year.

OCCURRENCE AND DISTRIBUTION:

Sequoia-Kings Canyon: Fairly common. Mid Sierra Zone.

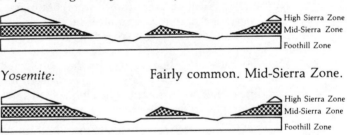

Yosemite: Fairly common. Mid-Sierra Zone.

Pocket Gopher

Thomomys ssp.

Dr. Joseph Grinnell, one-time professor at the University of California, once remarked that the farmers in the San Joaquin Valley were raising oranges and grapes on soil that pocket gophers dug up in the Sierra thousands of years ago. He was right, but to understand what he meant it is necessary to know how the animal lives.

The pocket gopher spends most of its life underground. It occasionally leaves its burrow at night, but it rarely comes out in the daytime, and then only on overcast days. It is especially adapted to its underground life. It has small, weak eyes, but living in total darkness most of the time, keen eyesight is of no importance. Its ears are short, a necessity for an animal living in tunnels not much larger than its body. Hearing does not appear to be acute, but its reaction to ground vibrations is instantaneous. Its whiskers act as feelers enabling it to follow even winding tunnels with great ease. Its tail, short and stubby with a sensitive tip, also serves as a guide, enabling it to run backward in its tunnels nearly as fast as it can run forward. To turn around in the narrow tunnel, it simply tucks its head between its hind legs, and, with a quick twisting motion, flips over and heads back the way it came.

The pocket gopher lives almost anywhere, but it prefers areas devoid of trees and where the soil is loose. It digs numerous tunnels, most of them only a few inches beneath the surface. As it digs, it disposes of the dirt by getting behind the loose material and "bulldozing" it to a surface exit. After several trips, a pile of dirt is spread on the ground around the hole. The final load is used to plug the exit. That way, no hungry bullsnake or kingsnake can find its way inside.

The piles of loose dirt brought to the surface by the gopher are rich in plant nutrients. Rains and melting snows move some of this dirt into small streams. Thence it is carried into the rivers that flow into the San Joaquin Valley. There, as in ages past, the dirt joins with the other soil to become part of the rich farmland. This, of course, is the basis for Dr. Grinnell's remark.

Digging tunnels is the means by which the gopher obtains its food. Life on the surface is dangerous, even at night,

and it spends no more time out of the protective tunnels than necessary. Instead it searches underground for roots, depending upon sense of smell to help locate them. When it finds one, it digs to the surface and either cuts the plant into manageable lengths or drags it down whole inside the tunnel. It may eat what it wants immediately, or it may stuff all the pieces of plant into its big, outside cheek pockets, and take them to one of its storerooms for future use. The gopher's den has many storage areas, and it is constantly making more. Frequently, the stored food molds or rots and is discarded, thus adding nutrients to the soil. The pocket gopher eats almost any kind of herb or bulb.

Mating takes place in late winter or early spring at a time when green vegetation is available. At that time, the males start out in search of mates, sometimes venturing out in broad daylight. Females stay in their dens. The male checks the various tunnels in an area until a mate is found. After mating he leaves and the female prepares her nest for the young. She then stocks her den with an ample supply of food to feed her family when it arrives. Usually there are four or five young. Their eyes and ears are sealed at birth. By the time six weeks have passed, they are ready to leave the nest and find their own homes. If a vacant burrow can be found, it is repaired by the new occupant; if not, it will dig a burrow of its own.

You would think that, living underground most of its life, the pocket gopher would be safe from predators. However, like so many small rodents, it is an important source of food for the badger, coyote, fox, skunk, bobcat, owls, and snakes. Some predators are able to dig it out; some surprise it on the surface; and snakes frequently invade the den if the pocket gopher is careless enough to leave a tunnel exit open for entry. Because it is active the year around, the pocket gopher is always in season for predators.

OCCURRENCE AND DISTRIBUTION:

Valley Pocket Gopher *(Thomomys bottae)*

Sequoia–Kings Canyon: Abundant generally. Foothill Zone into Mid-Sierra Zone.

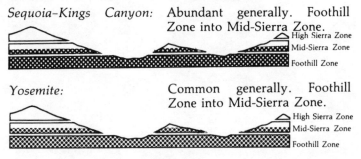

High Sierra Zone
Mid-Sierra Zone
Foothill Zone

Yosemite: Common generally. Foothill Zone into Mid-Sierra Zone.

High Sierra Zone
Mid-Sierra Zone
Foothill Zone

Sierra Pocket Gopher *(Thomomys monticola)*

Sequoia–Kings Canyon: Common. Mid-Sierra Zone into High Sierra Zone.

High Sierra Zone
Mid-Sierra Zone
Foothill Zone

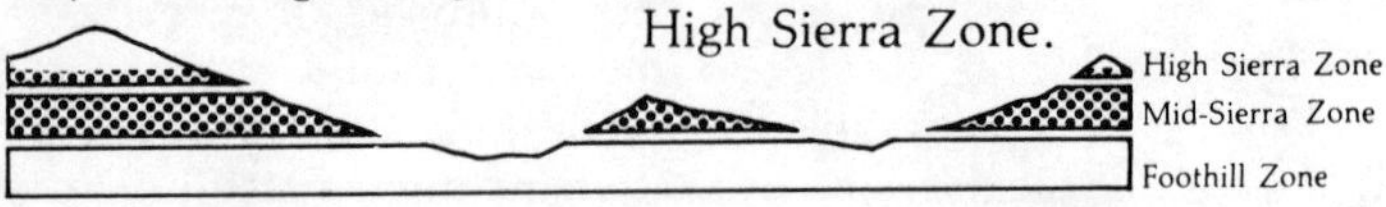

Yosemite: Common. Mid-Sierra Zone into High Sierra Zone.

High Sierra Zone
Mid-Sierra Zone
Foothill Zone

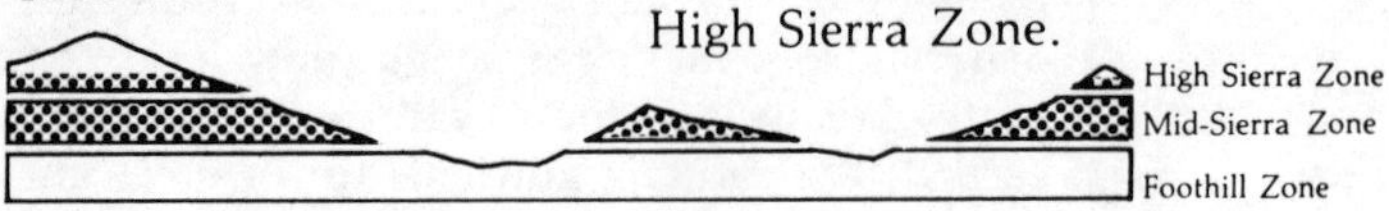

California Pocket Mouse

Perognathus californicus

It is a pity that one of the gentlest of the small mammals of the Sierra is one of the least likely to be seen. The pocket mouse is one of the few rodents that do not bite when it is picked up. It even seems to enjoy being handled. Add to that the fact that it is always clean and well-groomed, and you have a very appealing little creature. However, the pocket mouse is nocturnal and seldom seen in daylight. It lives in the parks at low elevations where most visitors do not stop to view the natural scenes or study wildlife.

The pocket mouse seems to have one compelling desire —to accumulate food. Even when food is abundant, it stores all it can get. When it finds a good supply of seeds or green food, it stuffs its two cheek pockets as full as possible in an incredibly short time, races away to a storage area, and returns immediately to get another load. It will eat most seeds, but particularly enjoys those of the aster family. In spring it enjoys tender green plants. Although it does not hibernate, it remains underground during much of the winter. The food stored during the summer can now be eaten leisurely within the protection of the burrow.

The pocket mouse does not require a large territory in which to live—just enough to provide it with sufficient food. A chaparral slope, with grass and other herbs in the openings, is its total world. Water is no problem. It obtains much of its needs from green vegetation, and uses the seeds it collects to produce additional moisture. Its burrow, which is not extensive, is usually located near the base of a shrub or at the side of a rock. Often it begins and ends under the same bush. From the surface, the burrow dips steeply. If the ground is soft and easy to dig, several looping tunnels may be constructed. This intricate network offers considerable protection should the mouse be threatened by an enemy small enough to invade the den. The sleeping room is usually on a short spur off the main tunnel. It is lined with fine grass, seed pods, or other plant materials. To discourage intruders, the pocket mouse plugs all the entrances to its den after finishing its nightly activities.

Enemies are numerous and the mouse has a dim life expectancy. If it survives a year, it is doing well, for it is subject to tremendous hunting pressures. Its enemies are skilled hunters and include the badger, weasel, coyote, fox, skunk, owls, and snakes. Besides all these it must also fear one of its own cousins—the white-footed mouse. This miniature predator kills and eats many pocket mice.

Because it is an important part of the food chain, the pocket mouse must raise large numbers of young each year in order to maintain a stable population level. It is solitary in its living habits, but the rule is broken during the mating season. This usually takes place twice a year, depending upon the mother mouse. Both litters of from four to six young are born during the warm months. Their stay with the mother is short. The young mice grow up quickly and are soon out establishing their own territories and burrows, working hard to lay away food for the coming winter.

OCCURRENCE AND DISTRIBUTION:

Sequoia–Kings Canyon.   Fairly common. Middle elevation of Foothill Zone.

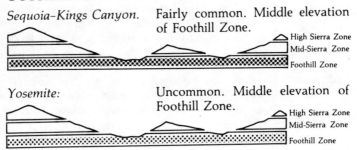

Yosemite: Uncommon. Middle elevation of Foothill Zone.

Beaver

Castor Canadensis

The beaver has several characteristics that set it apart from other Sierra mammals; three of these are of particular interest. It is the largest rodent in North America attaining a weight of as much as forty pounds. It builds a structure that affords protection against most of its enemies. It has a tail that serves as a stool, a rudder, an alarm system, and a diving plane when swimming. The beaver is also believed to be exotic to the Sierra. At one time it was common along the streams in the Great Central Valley of California, but not native to the mountains. Several years ago the California Department of Fish and Game introduced beaver into streams near the southwestern border of Yosemite. These later moved into part of the park. Still later, beaver moved into Sequoia from transplants made along the Kern River outside of the park.

The beaver dam is recognized as quite an engineering feat, although it usually starts out in a somewhat haphazard fashion. It begins by collecting sticks, rocks, mud, and fallen material of any kind, placing them into a narrow part of the stream. At first the water continues to flow through and around this barricade. But the beaver industriously plugs the weak points in the dam until it finally holds back enough water to form a small pond. The dam is now enlarged by working more sticks and debris into the structure. Over these it plasters mud, brought up from the bottom of the widening and deepening pond. This continues until the depth of the water and the size of the pond is sufficient to meet the beaver's needs.

The location for its lodge may be on shore, on a point of land rising above the level of the pond, or even in shallow water. In any event, the location of the lodge site must be near deep water in the pond. If it builds the lodge in shallow water, it must construct a foundation first. Again the beaver uses sticks, mud, and debris as his building materials. Soon the structure rises above the level of the pond, and the inside walls of the sleeping quarters are built, well plastered with mud. It also builds one or more doorways from the lodge into the water. From time to time, the beaver adds more sticks and mud, and the lodge may eventually grow to be as much as seven feet high and thirty feet across.

The male beaver and his mate sleep on the bare floor of their lodge, but after mating the sleeping quarters are often

enlarged and a bed of leaves, grass and soft bark is built in preparation for a family. Beavers are normally monogamous for life. Mating takes place in the winter and about four months later the young are born. The father now takes up temporary quarters, usually in a bank den. As a rule, there are three or four in a litter, although there may be as few as one or as many as six. The new arrivals are not tiny; indeed, they are about fifteen inches long, including the tail. Their eyes are open at birth and they have well-furred bodies. Young beavers grow rapidly, and they soon change from a milk diet to one of plants. Swimming seems to come naturally to them and before long they are ready to take an active part in family life. Their first task will be to help their parents store food. The adult beaver cuts a tree which will either fall or be dragged into the water. Now the little beavers go to work. They are still too small to handle large branches, but they industriously cut off twigs and carry them to the family food pile described below. The young stay with their parents until the next litter is raised. Then they will be forced out of the lodge when two years old. By this time they are fully mature and ready to build their own homes and raise their own families.

One of the peculiarities of the mating season is the making of "sign heaps." These are flattened, or conical, piles of mud several inches across put along the edges of the streams. Male and female beavers have musk glands that give off an odor believed to be a means of identification; some of this musk is put on the mud piles.

The beaver is always pictured cutting down trees for food, and indeed, trees are a primary source of food. It eats quantities of tree bark of aspen, cottonwood, willow and alder. However it is also fond of various herbs, roots, bulbs, buds and the new leaves of several different kinds of shrubs. In winter, especially, it may eat pine and fir bark and twigs. Trees and large shrubs are cut for its winter food supply. The food pile is put under water, deep enough to be below the ice level if the pond is in an area experiencing frigid cold. During the winter months, the beaver has only to swim to the food pile, cut off a short branch, and take it to the lodge to eat. The beaver has a transparent eyelid that closes when under water, allowing it to see without difficulty. It also has fleshy flaps that close behind the teeth; these allow it to gnaw while submerged without getting a mouthful of water. Once stripped of its bark, the discarded stick is either added to the lodge or to the dam.

The beaver has few enemies. However, if caught away from its watery sanctuary, it may fall victim to the coyote, wolverine, cougar, or bobcat. When menaced, it will dive. As it dives, the heart beat slows, the blood vessels in the legs contract, and additional blood is forced into the brain and other vital organs. This enables the beaver to remain under water for as long as five minutes. Occasionally there is a different cause of loss of life. This occurs when the beaver fails to calculate accurately where a tree it is cutting will fall, and so is killed.

People who tell the story of the beaver often stop short of its greatest contribution to the wildlife scene. That part of the story dealing with dam building and falling trees is familiar to everyone who views television or reads about wildlife. However, not everyone knows the end product of the beaver's efforts, as this is seldom mentioned.

The construction of the dam and the creation of the beaver pond bring about a complete change in habitat, and, with it, a profound impact on the animal life along and in the stream. As the pond forms, small land animals are flooded out of their homes and forced to locate elsewhere. In their place, a new community is formed. Aquatic insects and vegtation, salamanders, small fishes, wading birds, often waterfowl are attracted to the pond. Eventually the pond silts up, the beavers move on, and marshy land takes over, bringing with it still different plants and animals. Many a lush mountain meadow owes its existence to a family of beavers.

OCCURRENCE AND DISTRIBUTION:

Sequoia–Kings Canyon: Common locally in Kern Canyon. Foothill Zone into Mid-Sierra Zone.

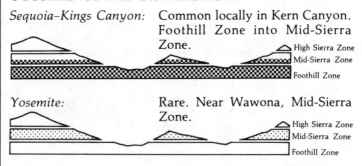

Yosemite: Rare. Near Wawona, Mid-Sierra Zone.

Western Harvest Mouse

Reithrodontomys megalotis

If you could hear all of the many sounds of nature, one that you would notice during the warm spring months is a shrill, high-pitched song coming from the grassy meadows in the lower elevations of the Sierra. In fact, this sound is nearly too high-pitched for the human ear to record. It is the song of the male harvest mouse, and it is usually heard during the mating season.

While the harvest mouse looks something like the familiar house mouse, it isn't closely related, nor does it have the same habits. It makes its home around meadows, especially along the borders, and in grassy openings among the oak and brushlands. Its choice of habitat is governed by food requirements and protection. Grasses not only provide much of its food, but also good ground cover. Its basket-sized nest is an oval structure that may be placed on the lower branches of a bush, or perhaps hidden in a large clump of grass. Occasionally it will take over a deserted woodpecker hole if not too high above the ground. Its nest is woven from grass stems and lined with soft grass and shredded plants. The female makes this lining even softer and warmer when she prepares to mate and raise her young.

While most mating activities take place in spring and late summer, the mother mouse may raise a family almost any time of the year. She normally has two, and sometimes three litters a year, each numbering from two to seven young. The average litter numbers four or five. Following mating, the expectant mother has only about three weeks to await the birth of her babies. The young mice are born blind and their ears are sealed. They begin to show a little fur when they are two days old. By the time they are a week old, their eyes and ears are open and they are growing rapidly. Amazingly, they are weaned when they are only two weeks old, and about two weeks later they leave the nest and start out to build their own.

The diet of the harvest mouse does not include a great variety of foods. For the most part it is made up of seeds, although some green grass tips are eaten when available. It will also eat insects such as moths, if it can catch them. It searches for food at night and usually eats the seeds as it finds them, though occasionally it stores some for future use. This is not a common practice, however, as the mouse den has no established storerooms.

Like other small rodents, the world of the harvest mouse is full of enemies, and only its ability to raise large numbers of young enables it to maintain a stable population. Foxes, weasels, coyotes, skunks, ringtails, hawks, owls, and several kinds of snakes are constant threats. If the mouse is alert and agile, it may survive for a year or more, but for most harvest mice the end comes sooner.

OCCURRENCE AND DISTRIBUTION:

Sequoia–Kings Canyon: Rare. Extreme lower elevation. Foothill Zone.

Yosemite: Rare. One record near the Cascades. Foothill Zone.

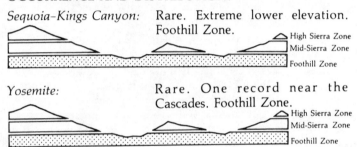

White-Footed Mouse

(Deer Mouse)
Peromyscus spp.

From the blazing heat on the floor of Death Valley to the snow fields of the high mountains—if food is there, the white-footed mouse will be there, too. It is found in heavy forests, brushy areas, around rocky cliffs, and even in houses —nearly everywhere except in cities and towns. It is the most abundant mammal in North America.

Campgrounds are popular places with the white-footed mouse. There it can find bread crumbs, bits of cookies, and other tidbits campers brush off of their tables. If it doesn't find food on the ground, it doesn't hesitate to do a bit of exploring during the night, looking into food boxes and the like. Being a good climber, it can easily reach a high shelf to find out what is stored there.

This mouse is a pretty creature, and immaculate in its appearance. It bathes and combs its fur often during the day. However such cleanliness is not reflected in the way it takes care of its nest. Apparently it enjoys eating in bed, and it scatters husks of seeds and bits of other discarded food all around in the sleeping area. Every so often the mouse simply leaves all the mess behind and builds a new nest.

It has a very unusual accomplishment—it can sing! Though its song is much like that of the harvest mouse, it cannot be described as musical. It is a shrill, buzzing sound that continues for several seconds and is audible for about fifty feet. No one really knows why it sings, although it is thought to be associated with the mating season. It has another interesting habit of drumming on the ground with its forefeet if something disturbs it. This sound can be heard for several yards.

Most individuals are solitary, with each mouse establishing its own territory and fighting off any intruders. Occasionally two mice may share the same nest during the winter.

In the spring, the male goes searching for a mate. When she is found, the courtship is brief, and the male departs,

leaving the female to raise the young. These arrive twenty-one to twenty-five days later. Litters are usually large, with as many as six to eight young. At birth, the babies are pink, naked, almost transparent, blind, and deaf. For the first two weeks, they grow rapidly. They remain blind for another week while the mother prepares to wean them. At the end of five weeks, they are sufficiently mature to face life on their own. Some of the young females will bear their own families by the time they are eight weeks old. A mature female may have as many as eight or more litters a year.

Its food includes a wide variety of seeds, fruits and green herbs. It prefers to hunt on the darkest nights, shunning the moonlight which would reveal the tiny creature to its many enemies. On moonlight nights, it stays in its nest until the moon has set; only then will it venture out. It brings some food back to the den to be stored for winter use when food becomes scarce. It likes meat and has been known to kill and eat other mice.

Enemies include about any predator that is a meat eater. The mouse is an important link in the food chain for such animals as the fox, coyote, bobcat, weasel, marten, badger, hawk, owl, and snake. It is an old mouse that survives for a year and most live only six months. Without the prolific birth rate, the mouse population would soon be much reduced.

Four different species of white-footed mouse are found in the three parks.

OCCURRENCE AND DISTRIBUTION:

Brush Mouse *(Peromyscus boylii)*
Sequoia–Kings Canyon: Uncommon. Foothill Zone into Mid-Sierra Zone.

Yosemite: Uncommon. Foothill Zone into Mid-Sierra Zone.

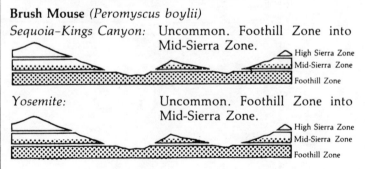

California Mouse *(Peromyscus californicus)*
Sequoia–Kings Canyon: Rare. Southern sector, Foothill Zone.

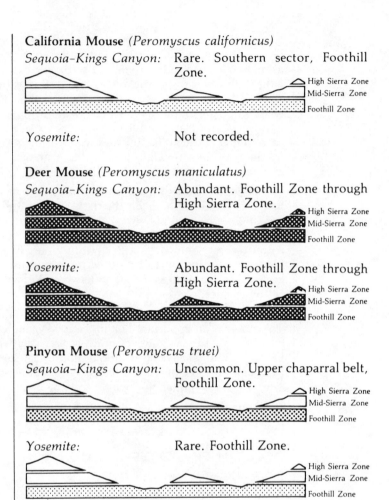

Yosemite: Not recorded.

Deer Mouse *(Peromyscus maniculatus)*
Sequoia–Kings Canyon: Abundant. Foothill Zone through High Sierra Zone.

Yosemite: Abundant. Foothill Zone through High Sierra Zone.

Pinyon Mouse *(Peromyscus truei)*
Sequoia–Kings Canyon: Uncommon. Upper chaparral belt, Foothill Zone.

Yosemite: Rare. Foothill Zone.

Woodrat

(Trade Rat, Pack Rat, Miner's Rat)
Neotoma spp.

Most animals spend the major part of their waking hours trying to get enough food to fill their stomachs, raising young, making dens, and keeping from being eaten. The woodrat does all these things, but in addition it finds time to collect all manner of things which it brings to its den. More than one camper has awakened in the morning to find that some of his prized possessions are missing. Not being particularly afraid of humans while they are asleep, the woodrat visits campsites and investigates everything of interest. Any small object, such as a coin, a ring, a spoon, or a bottle cap left in view, may be carried away to add to the woodrat's collection. No one knows why the woodrat collects things, but it usually brings something to its den every night. One nest near a campground, was found to contain part of a comic sheet, a piece of cellophane, a cigar band, an empty cigarette pack, several paper clips, two nails, and several common pins!

On its nocturnal hunt for food, the woodrat seldom goes far before finding something interesting to pack along. This may be a shiny pebble, a piece of bark, part of a pine cone—anything. If it should find something else attractive, it discards the first treasure for the new one. The last item it is carrying when it heads for its sleeping quarters usually ends up in the nest, or on the pile of debris it calls home. This trait has earned it several names, including "pack rat" and "trade rat."

The woodrat's home is not a thing of beauty, but it does give it a good place to live. It may be located anywhere that strikes the animal's fancy—on the ground, in the brush, under a rocky ledge, even in an oak tree. One nest found in an old deserted cabin in Kings Canyon was nearly circular, more than six feet across and two feet high. It was made of all sorts of material—sticks, twigs, bark, small rocks, and bits of debris. Three floor-level doorways furnished entrances into the den, and the size of the pile indicated that it had been accumulating for several years, and that probably more than one occupant had helped build it.

The woodrat mates in late winter, and the young, usu-

ally two or three in a litter, are born about a month later in April or May. One litter per season is normal, but occasionally there are more. The babies are blind and deaf, and not until more than two weeks have passed can they see or hear the world around them. In the third week they are weaned, and their diet changes to solid food. Soon they are large enough to leave the nest and locate their own territories, sometimes at some distance from their first home. Perhaps a deserted woodrat nest nearby requires only a little renovating to be considered liveable.

Most of the woodrat's food is vegetable matter. It is very fond of acorns, various seeds, currants and manzanita berries, and several kinds of green foliage. It eats most of its food where it is found, but it does bring considerable quantities back to its den to eat in greater safety. Some may be stored for later use.

Enemies are numerous, and the woodrat must be constantly alert to survive. Coyotes, foxes, weasels, bobcats, hawks, and owls are always on the lookout hoping to catch it away from its den. The ringtail is especially feared. Snakes, such as the gopher snake and kingsnake, are efficient hunters as they can follow the woodrat into its home. An entire woodrat family may be eliminated by one such visit.

The woodrat occupies an important place in the ecology of the area in which it lives. Not only is it a valuable source of food for predators, but it also contributes to the plant and animal community by enriching the soil near its den with abundant droppings. Its home is shared with spiders, mites, larvae of several kinds, small lizards, and a great assortment of insects. The mass of debris in its home rots down, helping to form rich, new soil where plants thrive.

The Sierra offers the types of habitats that are so essential to the woodrat's existence, and three different species have adapted themselves to various elevations, establishing their respective territories all the way from the foothills to the high mountains.

OCCURRENCE AND DISTRIBUTION:

Bushytail Woodrat *(Neotoma cinerea)*

Sequoia–Kings Canyon and Yosemite: Common. Upper Mid-Sierra Zone into High Sierra Zone.

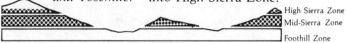

High Sierra Zone
Mid-Sierra Zone
Foothill Zone

Desert Woodrat *(Neotoma lepida)*

Sequoia–Kings Canyon: Rare. One record from the Giant Forest. Mid-Sierra Zone.

High Sierra Zone
Mid-Sierra Zone
Foothill Zone

Yosemite: Not recorded.

Dusky-footed Woodrat *(Neotoma fuscipes)*

Sequoia–Kings Canyon: Common in chaparral and blue oak belt. Foothill Zone.

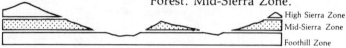

High Sierra Zone
Mid-Sierra Zone
Foothill Zone

Yosemite: Common. Foothill Zone.

High Sierra Zone
Mid-Sierra Zone
Foothill Zone

Meadow Mouse
Microtus spp.

Park meadows may appear deserted during the day, except perhaps for an occasional bird. Deer are bedded down and won't be feeding until late in the day. Nothing seems to move. But these silent meadows actually teem with life. A search among the grasses will disclose a network of well-hidden little trails going everywhere but leading nowhere in particular. Such are the evidences that you are in the home territory of one or several of the small voles we call the meadow mice.

A meadow mouse rivals the shrew in its fierce activity. It is busy day and night, rushing about, searching for food enough to satisfy its voracious appetite. It consumes its own weight in food about every twenty-four hours, and this requires a lot of running around. To reach its food and, at the same time to obtain some protection, it works its way through the meadow grasses, snipping off stems and making a path as it goes. This path soon becomes well traveled, and, as time goes by, it cuts spur trails to reach other feeding areas. These may connect with still other paths until there is an extensive network. While each mouse makes these trails primarily for its own use, they are often used by other meadow mice in the area.

The meadow mouse lives close to others of its kind, but it prefers to live alone in its own territory. It gets along well with its neighbors, but should one invade its territory, there is almost certain to be a fight. Though food may become scarce, it will not leave its chosen territory to search for something to eat. Faced with starvation, it simply accepts the situation and survives as long as any food is available. This behavior seems strange, but it does tend to reduce the danger of mass starvation of all mice in the meadow should numbers in one area increase beyond the available food resources of that area. This sometimes happens when predator pressures are insufficient to take care of the high birth rate.

In the summer, if the soil is dry, the meadow mouse builds its nest underground. Its home is an intricate network of tunnels as complex as the surface trails. Entrance into these tunnels is via small, round holes located under grass clumps, sticks, or debris. As it digs its tunnels, the mouse

moves the loose dirt up to the surface and leaves it there in flattened piles. It has been suggested that the mouse goes underground in the summer to escape the heat, but it appears just as likely it does so to hide from predators. If the soil is wet, it builds a nest in a clump of grass. In the winter it tunnels under the snow and builds a nest on the ground.

Its food is almost anything that is edible. It collects seeds whenever they are available, and eagerly seeks the tender bulbs of brodiaea or lily. It likes the tender cambium layer beneath the bark of trees and shrubs, and many such plants may be seen that have been attacked by gnawing away the bark. This mouse will also eat anything it can kill, nor is it adverse to dining on carrion. Its enormous appetite is sometimes quite beneficial, for it will dig up and eat the pupae of several destructive forest insects, thus helping to keep down their numbers.

The mother mouse breeds throughout the year and may produce ten or more litters. To prepare for her first litter, she finds an area where the grass grows in thick clumps, and here she weaves her nest, a hollow, ball-like structure of grasses or sedge, lined with moss or some other soft material. If she cannot find a suitable location above ground, she will use a simple underground burrow. The new-born young, usually between five and nine in number, start life entirely hairless, blind, and deaf. However, their development is astonishingly rapid. Fur begins to appear the first day, and the eyes and ears open about a week later. By the time the young mouse is two weeks old, it has grown enough to nibble on tender, green plant shoots and obtain most of its own food. At this stage, the mother promptly weans it. While she is still taking care of her first family, she mates again. The new litter will arrive in twenty-one days, and she must prepare for their coming. This means her present brood must soon strike out on its own. The young females of the brood begin to breed when they are about two months old. Small wonder that meadow mice can, if unchecked, quickly over-populate an area in a very short time. The normal mouse population is about thirty per acre of land. However, the population in any given area tends to double and redouble about every four years. As many as a thousand mice may thus occupy a single acre. When this happens, only starvation, hunting pressure, disease—or perhaps all three—will drop their numbers back down to normal.

This ability to raise large numbers of young insures the survival of the meadow mouse, which is important, for it is one of Nature's most efficient converters of energy. Its enemies include every predator, from the large mammals, such as the bobcat, coyote and fox, down to the smallest, including the fierce little shrew. Hawks, owls, ravens, and several kinds of snakes eat dozens of these mice during the summer. The life expectancy of a mouse is grim. If it survives a year, it is fortunate—if for as much as eighteen months, it is an old animal! Each time it ventures from its underground home, in search of food, the chances are strong that it will furnish a meal for a predator rather than gain one for itself.

Finding a meadow mouse requires patience, sharp eyes and quiet. Almost any meadow contains several, and you need only to locate the network of used trails, and then watch patiently until a mouse appears. Because it is always in a hurry, your glimpse may be brief!

Two species of meadow mouse are known to occur in the Sierra. A third—the California Meadow Mouse—is found in the low valleys and may enter all three parks in the Foothill Zone.

OCCURRENCE AND DISTRIBUTION:

Longtail Meadow Mouse *(Microtus longicaudus)*

Sequoia–Kings Canyon and Yosemite: Common. Mid-Sierra and High Sierra Zones.

High Sierra Zone
Mid-Sierra Zone
Foothill Zone

Mountain Meadow Mouse *(Microtus montanus)*

Sequoia–Kings Canyon: Uncommon. One record in southern sector near Mt. Whitney, High Sierra Zone.

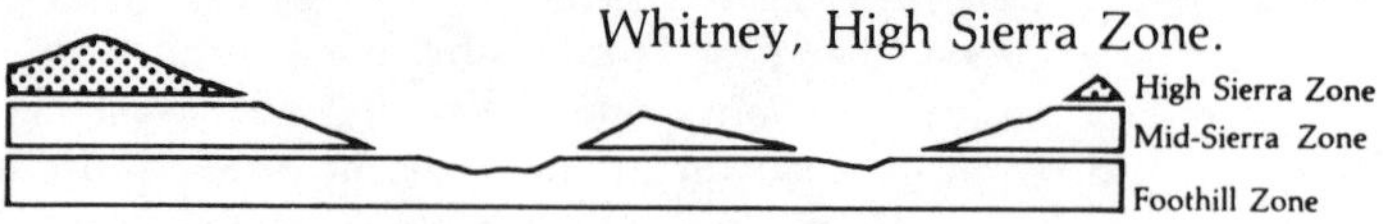

High Sierra Zone
Mid-Sierra Zone
Foothill Zone

Heather
Vole

Phenacomys intermedius

This hardy little creature lives in the higher elevations, and thus must face short summers and long winters. There may be ample food in the warmer months, but only a limited supply when snow covers the ground. It is found in open, grassy areas near mountain tops, but it prefers to live in or around large clumps of red heather. Not only does this plant afford excellent protection, but its new spring and summer growth is edible. It also has a strong liking for old fire burns, likely because such areas produce large quantities of small green plants and an abundance of seeds. The highland forests, rocky slopes and even dry areas away from water are used. Other foods include berries, lichen and willow bark. Any food items not eaten immediately are brought back to its den and stored for future use.

During the summer months, the vole builds its nest above ground, choosing places where digging is easy, such as around rocks, beneath old stumps, and in piles of forest debris. Unlike its close relative, the meadow mouse, it does not make a vast network of trails. Its presence is nearly unnoticeable and only sharp eyes will enable a person to find its home.

The vole does not produce the vast numbers of young so characteristic of the meadow mouse. This may be partly because there is not the hunting pressure from predators experienced by other species of mice at lower elevations. Even so, it must be alert constantly to escape such skilled hunters as the weasel, marten, fisher and bobcat. However, few of these are found where the vole lives.

Mating usually takes place in May or June, and there may be two or more litters before the fall arrives. While the young may be born at any time in the year, most appear from June to September when food is relatively abundant. The mother may prepare for the arrival of her family by building a nest on the ground, or she may decide to use a nearby tree. If a tree is chosen, she selects a place where the foliage is heavy and a number of small branches form a clump. There she constructs a nest of small twigs and needles. Sometimes she cleans up an old chickaree nest and uses that. If the nest is placed on the ground, it will be well hidden with grass comprising the usual nesting materials. Nests have been found near the 11,000 foot (3360m) level in Yosemite, indicating that the vole lives close to the upper limits of available food.

The young are born twenty-one days after mating. Normally there are five or six young to a litter, and they arrive entirely hairless, blind and deaf. Hair appears on the young vole only a few hours after birth. Growth is rapid, and only a few days pass before it is fully furred and its eyes and ears are open. Soon it begins to sample various plants along with its milk diet. It matures quickly and is able to take care of itself by the end of the fifth week. Young females mate by the time they are six weeks old and raise at least one litter during their first year.

OCCURRENCE AND DISTRIBUTION:

Sequoia–Kings Canyon: Rare. High Sierra Zone, northern region.

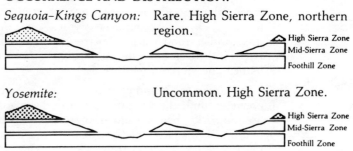

Yosemite: Uncommon. High Sierra Zone.

Western Jumping Mouse
Zapus princeps

Your first encounter with a jumping mouse is likely to be an astonishing one. While walking along the edge of a moist meadow or in heavy vegetation near a stream or spring, you may have a small, golden-brown and white ball explode into the air from beneath your feet as though hurled into space by a spring. In rapid succession it makes a number of long jumps, sometimes six feet or more, zig-zagging as it goes. When it feels it has put a safe distance between itself and the intruder, it remains motionless among the grass or other vegetation for several minutes, its coloration making it extremely difficult to see. It does not run and hide like other mice do when alarmed. When all danger appears to have passed, it goes on with its interrupted activity. If it is near a stream it may take to the water to escape, as it can swim readily.

The jumping mouse doesn't build trails through the grassy jungle in which it lives. This is because it is rather awkward when it tries to walk and would have a difficult time getting through the tangle of plant stems. Rather, it has adapted to its environment by developing long legs which propel it through the air and over obstacles with ease. Equally important as its legs is its long, slender tail with a small tuft of hair on the tip. This serves as its balancing mechanism. Without the tail to guide it through the air and to assist in making a smooth landing, the jumping mouse would be nearly helpless.

Its home is a round or cone-shaped nest built on the ground in the midst of dense vegetation, making it difficult to see. Sometimes it digs a shallow cup in the ground and places the nest inside. It is made of grass, bits of leaves, and other small pieces of vegetation. A small opening on one side leads into a bedroom about two to three inches in diameter. This is its summer home, and there are no trails leading to the nest that would disclose its presence to its enemies. In the fall, its housing needs change, for unlike other species of mice, the jumping mouse hibernates. It prepares for its winter sleep by digging a burrow deep enough to protect it

from the winter cold. Here it constructs a warm nest where it will sleep until spring arrives. It is solitary, except for a short period during the mating season which occurs soon after it emerges from hibernation. Immediately thereafter the female resumes her solitary life. About a month later—a long period for a mouse— the young are usually born in June or early July. The young number about five or six, and are born blind and without fur. At birth, the mouse's tail is short, but it grows very rapidly after the first week. After six weeks, the young mouse is mature enough to leave the nest, establish its territory, and build its own nest. For the most part, this is not difficult, as territories are not defended by others of its kind and it can easily claim a small area for its own.

The jumping mouse may forage for food in the daytime, but it is primarily a nocturnal animal. It eats all kinds of seeds, with grasses furnishing the major share. It gathers seeds by pulling the grasshead over until the seeds can be reached from the ground, or by cutting the stem of the plant. It does not store its food, as do other mice, but eats almost everything on the spot, although it may stuff a tidbit into its cheeks to take along to eat at a more leisurely time. Its primary objective is to put on as much fat as possible in preparation for its long winter sleep. Often it becomes so heavy that it can hardly move.

Its enemies are the predators commonly found in the evergreen forests, with the fox, marten, weasel and owl the most to be feared. The jumping mouse is not an important prey species. Consequently, it suffers less from hunting pressures than do other mouse species, and its population remains fairly stable from year to year.

OCCURRENCE AND DISTRIBUTION:

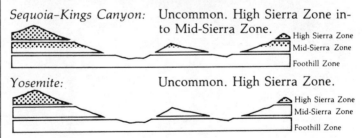

Sequoia–Kings Canyon: Uncommon. High Sierra Zone into Mid-Sierra Zone.

High Sierra Zone
Mid-Sierra Zone
Foothill Zone

Yosemite: Uncommon. High Sierra Zone.

High Sierra Zone
Mid-Sierra Zone
Foothill Zone

Porcupine

(Quill Pig)
Erethizon dorsatum

No animal in the Sierra faces life in a more placid, serene manner than the porcupine. Most mammals are constantly on the alert for danger when outside their dens, becoming nervous at the slightest unexplained sound, and panicking when danger threatens. Not so the porcupine. It goes its way slowly plodding, paying little attention to anything not resembling food. It seldom knows danger is near until too late to run. Running wouldn't really help much as it moves slowly. Only when it feels threatened does it take measures to protect itself. However, stupid as it may seem to be, it has some positive and effective answers when attacked.

The porcupine, "quill pig," or simply "porky," is a walking forest of sharp spears. It has been estimated to carry as many as twenty to thirty thousand quills of various sizes. These are mostly hidden in the long, coarse hair that covers most of its body. The quills may vary in length. Those on the back and tail sometimes reach a length of two inches, while those on the sides and head are about an inch long. Each quill is slender, hollow, rather stiff and with an exceptionally sharp point. Near the point of the quill are numerous tiny, black barbs, something like the barb on a fish-hook. When driven into the flesh of an attacker, the quill works its way deeper and deeper, and may eventually penetrate into a vital organ, causing great damage or even death. The quill is almost impossible to pull out once the barbs begin their work. As quills are lost or fall out, others grow in to replace them.

When faced with danger, the porcupine suddenly erects its quills, creating a formidable shield that few animals will attempt to penetrate. At the same time, it swings its club-like tail from side to side as a warning, and makes low, chattering sounds with its teeth. It turns its head away from its would-be attacker, always presenting its humped back and threatening tail. Any animal too inexperienced or rash as to heed these warnings and gets too close, will receive a lightning-quick slap with the tail and a quantity of quills in the process. Not surprisingly few animals will face the threat of these barbed spears, so the porcupine is seldom under attack. It can be killed, however, if the attacker can reach its unprotected stomach or throat. The coyote, bobcat, fisher and mountain lion occasionally try to flip the porcupine on its back, and are sometimes successful. Even these skilled hunters sometimes receive a painful lesson. Man has become one of the greatest threats faced by the porcupine. Many are killed by cars while crossing the roads, especially at night.

While the porcupine usually has a place it calls home, it is often away for considerable periods of time. It may live almost anywhere—in a hollow log, a shallow cave, or among the jumbled rocks of a talus slope. It seldom gets very far from its den, and returns at irregular intervals.

The porcupine does most of its foraging at night, and usually finds plenty to eat. It is often pictured strictly as a bark-eater, but such is not the case. It does enjoy quantities of the tender inner bark of such evergreens as the ponderosa pine and fir, especially during the winter months. Cottonwood, aspen, alder, and willow are also important items in its diet, and it will often climb into one of these trees and remain there for several days, eating and sleeping, as the mood strikes it. But it eats many other things as well. These include the fresh green leaves of the currant, gooseberry, deerbush, and several kinds of herbs. One odd food item, when it can be found, is a discarded deer antler. This probably furnishes needed minerals, and the porcupine is very fond of chewing on the bone.

The family life of the porcupine begins in the fall, when mating takes place. About six months later, in April or May, a single baby is born. The mother makes no special nest for this event, and the baby may be born in any convenient shelter. It arrives well prepared to take care of itself, with heavy, black fur and hundreds of tiny quills, already developed and ready for action as soon as they dry. By the time it is two days old, it can climb, which affords it some additional protection. Though it is soon weaned and able to feed itself, it does not leave its mother to start its own solitary life until it is around six months old. By that time, it is almost fully mature.

Often the question is asked: "What good is a porcupine? It kills trees and isn't of much value as a food." It does kill a few trees each year, but dead trees have a real value in Nature. They become nesting sites for woodpeckers and homes for various insects, and eventually rot down and help to enrich the soil. Certainly it isn't an important food source, but it is an interesting part of the wildlife scene. We would be that much poorer if it weren't here for us to see.

OCCURRENCE AND DISTRIBUTION:

Sequoia–Kings Canyon: Uncommon. High Sierra Zone into Mid-Sierra Zone.

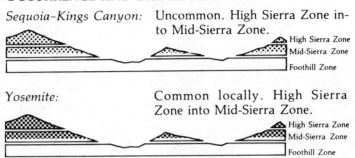

Yosemite: Common locally. High Sierra
Zone into Mid-Sierra Zone.

The Rabbits and their Relatives

These are important members of the food chain. They are eaten by all the predatory mammals, and by some birds and reptiles as well. Like the rodents, they are able to keep their population levels high through their ability to raise many young.

Pika

(Rock-rabbit, Cony)
Ochotona princeps

A sharp, high-pitched "chek-ak" coming from a jumbled pile of broken rock is the usual introduction to the pika (pronounced peek-ah). The call is repeated several times, each time seeming to come from nowhere in particular. It isn't until a tiny, rabbit-like creature perched on top of a rock is finally seen that the source of the calls becomes evident.

The color and form of the pika blend so well with the gray and brown rocks where it lives that it is very difficult to distinguish. As it sits watching you, only the head moves. The series of calls is a danger signal, uttered by the first pika in the neighborhood to discover an approaching intruder. At the sound of this alarm call, another pika in the vicinity finds a good observation point and becomes a lookout, his sharp warning call continues the alarm until he feels danger is too near. Then, in a flash, he disappears among the rocks. Farther away, the warning is repeated by still other pikas. This continues until the intruder has gone. Sometimes it is possible to get reasonably close to a pika by moving slowly and talking to it softly. A lack of menace in the voice seems to reassure the timid animal.

The pika has several other names by which it is known. It is often called a "cony" which is a misnomer, for the cony is a European rabbit. It is also called a "rock-rabbit—somewhat more accurately since it is closely related to the cottontail. Very descriptive, and also very appropriate, is another common name: "little haymaker." This name refers to one of its best known traits—that of making hay.

The pika's diet consists of various kinds of plants. Some of these it eats when it is cut fresh, some of which is sun-cured. As it seldom finds all the plants it needs amid the piles of jumbled rocks where it lives, it must sometimes go several yards from home to get its food. With furry soles on its feet, it can dash without noise through and over its rocky domain to get to the plants it wants, usually without being detected. In late summer and early fall, it cuts considerable quantities of grasses, flowers, leaves, and small stems and carries them to the shelter of the rocks. It uses practically every kind of plant in the vicinity. Like a farmer making hay it lays out the cut plants among the rocks where they are exposed to the drying warmth of the sun. Day by day, the hay pile grows until by the time the first snows come, it contains a rather large quantity of dried plants. Often it makes several such piles. Because the pika lives in the higher elevations, a good food pile is important, because once snow begins to fall it no longer has access to the plant fields. It must now exist during the winter on the hay it has sun cured. It does not hibernate in the winter, but simply spends most of its time eating and sleeping, deep in its rocky home. We know little about its winter life, but apparently it has social visits from other pikas in the neighborhood, although it is doubtful that any food from the haypile is shared.

Its breeding habits and home life are not well known. The young, numbering three or four, are born from late May to September. They grow rapidly and are weaned and ready to live on plant life by the time they are a third grown. When nearly full grown, they scatter to find their own living quarters and territories.

While the pika has few enemies, it must be constantly on the alert to escape what it has. Most of its problems of survival occur in the summer. The lack of snow enables such relentless hunters as the weasel and marten to scour the rock slides in search of a pika home. Occasionally a hawk is successful in surprising a pika when it is moving about or taking a sun bath on an exposed rock. It lives at altitudes too cold for snakes. With so few enemies the pika population might be expected to become dangerously high, but it never does. It is probable that the amount of food that can be reached safely has a limiting effect upon its numbers, while predators take care of any surplus. Whatever the reason, the pika continues to thrive from year to year—a common and most delightful animal.

OCCURRENCE AND DISTRIBUTION:

Sequoia–Kings Canyon: Common. High Sierra Zone into Mid-Sierra Zone.

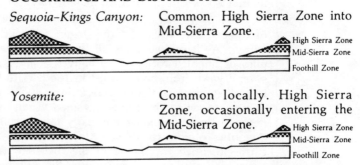

High Sierra Zone
Mid-Sierra Zone
Foothill Zone

Yosemite: Common locally. High Sierra Zone, occasionally entering the Mid-Sierra Zone.

High Sierra Zone
Mid-Sierra Zone
Foothill Zone

Jackrabbit
Lepus spp.

The jackrabbit looks like an oversize cottontail with exceptionally long ears. Actually it is not a rabbit at all, but a close relative—the hare. There are several differences between the rabbit and the hare, one of the most important being that the young rabbit is born blind, while the young hare is born with its eyes open.

The jackrabbit is well known for its speed. If disturbed, it takes off with long, easy bounds, but can quickly accelerate to as much as thirty-five miles an hour or more. It may sit quietly in its form (a shallow, bowl-like depression it makes in the ground) until an intruder gets close, or it may see what is approaching and is able to leave before danger threatens. A bobcat or coyote may be momentarily too startled to react if a jackrabbit suddenly explodes under its nose, allowing the jackrabbit to gain valuable ground before a footrace begins. Even if the coyote musters enough speed to get close, the jackrabbit may elude it by zig-zagging at high speed. Unless the coyote draws uncomfortably close, the jackrabbit bounds high every few leaps in order to keep tabs on its pursuer. As it runs, it lays back its sensitive ears to protect them from being damaged by bushes. The huge ears are essential for its safety, and the membranes so delicate and thin that the jackrabbit cannot risk getting them torn.

The jackrabbit's territorial requirements are modest. An area a couple of miles across is about as much as it finds necessary to supply all of its needs. Normally it spends the day sitting in a well protected spot, and does not venture out until the sun is setting. It feeds mostly at night, and dawn finds it ready to return to its form—or to another one, for it maintains several of these resting places. It eats all sorts of vegetation. Leaves, twigs, buds, the bark of shrubs, and sometimes plants are welcome—but its favorite foods are grass and flowers. Hay growing in the low valleys of the Sierra is certain to attract large numbers of jackrabbits.

Mating activities are not restricted to one season of the year. The female may mate anytime from early spring until well into the summer months. Battles between rival males are common. Sometimes these become quite violent, leaving the ground littered with bits of fur. After mating, the male leaves, and the female prepares to raise her family. Beneath an overhanging bush or a clump of grass, she digs a shallow de-

pression. She lines this with fur pulled from her own body. The young are born fully furred, and the litter may range in number between two and seven. The ears, soon to become the most prominent feature of the animal, are small at birth, but they grow rapidly. Each day while the young are still very small, the mother feeds them, covers them with grass or bits of her fur, and then moves off a short distance to another form. Here she settles down to watch over her family. She will not visit them again until dark, as she might give away the location of her babies. As soon as the young can eat tender plant tips and grass blades, they quickly become independent of her care, and soon they begin to drift away on their own. This is a critical time for them, for they are inexperienced in caring for themselves and they have many enemies.

With the departure of this family, the mother may raise one or more additional litters before the summer is over. Because so many young are born each year, there is an ever-increasing breeding population. Unless checked they will overproduce. Their numbers soon skyrocket and do not return to normal until hunting pressures by predators, disease, lack of adequate food, or all three in combination, cause a rapid decline. This rise and fall in population seems to be cyclic and occurs about every seven years.

The jackrabbit is faced with two important dilemmas. Outside the parks, it is often killed by man, especially in the lower valleys where it frequently does considerable damage to farmers' crops. In the mountains of the Sierra, it is an important link in the food chain leading to the large predators. In spite of its enemies, the jackrabbit continues to maintain a steady population over most of its range.

Two species of hares—both jackrabbits—are found in the Sierran parks. A third species, the Snowshoe Rabbit *(Lepus americanus)*, is known to occur north of Yosemite and may enter the northern part of the park.

OCCURRENCE AND DISTRIBUTION:

Blacktail Jackrabbit *(Lepus californicus)*

Sequoia–Kings Canyon: Uncommon. Foothill Zone into Mid-Sierra Zone.

High Sierra Zone
Mid-Sierra Zone
Foothill Zone

Yosemite: Uncommon. Foothill Zone into Mid-Sierra Zone.

High Sierra Zone
Mid-Sierra Zone
Foothill Zone

Whitetail Jackrabbit *(Lepus townsendii)*

Sequoia–Kings Canyon: Uncommon. High Sierra Zone.

High Sierra Zone
Mid-Sierra Zone
Foothill Zone

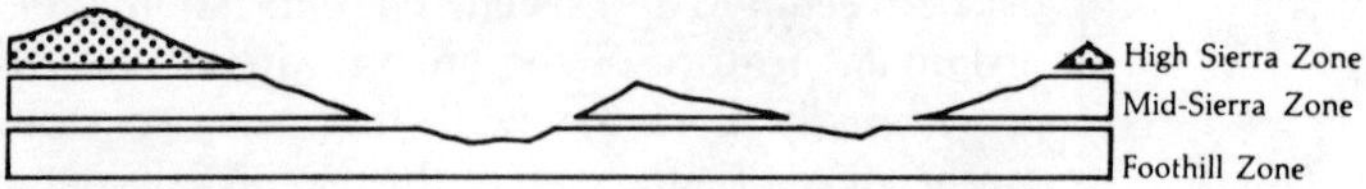

Yosemite: Common. High Sierra Zone.

High Sierra Zone
Mid-Sierra Zone
Foothill Zone

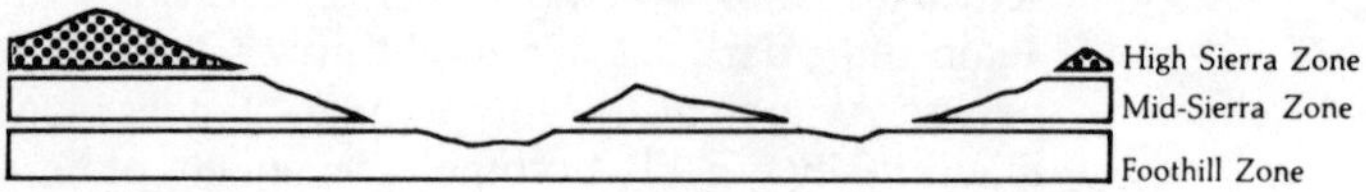

Cottontail Rabbit

Sylvilagus spp.

The rabbit is surely one of the best known of all the mammals in this country. Scores of children's stories have been written about "Peter Rabbit." The Indians made the rabbit an important character in their legends. The Uncle Remus story "Tarbaby and Brer Fox" is actually derived from one such legend. Most of these stories had one feature in common—the rabbit is always getting into trouble, and always in danger of being killed. These accounts are only stories, but they usually stress a real fact—the rabbit is one of the most hunted animals in the wild. There are many kinds of predators that depend upon the rabbit as a primary food. The coyote, various kinds of foxes, bobcat, weasels, hawks, owls, and snakes are always where rabbits live—whether in the mountains, in the woodlands, or in the valleys and plains. In addition, the marten and fisher of the Sierra take their toll. Certainly the rabbit occupies an unenviable position in the food chain, and the individual faces a very brief existence. As though this were not enough, man and his gun kill millions yearly as does his destructive cars.

With so many enemies, the rabbit might be expected to be threatened with extinction. However, like other small mammals that serve as suppliers of food, nature has given the rabbit the ability to produce large numbers of young each year, so the population remains fairly stable.

To maintain a strong population, the rabbit breeds several times a year. The mating season runs from February until late summer. Mating often begins in an almost humorous fashion. A pair of rabbits face each other a few feet apart. Then one leaps high into the air while the other runs under it. They may repeat this routine several times. Sometimes more than one male becomes involved and a fight results. Soon after she has accepted a mate, the female chases him away and will have nothing more to do with him, as the male is not allowed around when the young are born. The young are born twenty-eight to thirty days after mating. To prepare for this event, the mother selects a suitable place for a nest three or four days before her babies are due. The nesting site may be almost anywhere—in the brush, in a meadow, or simply in the midst of a large clump of grass.

Here she digs a shallow, bowl-shaped depression which she lines with soft grass and fur pulled from her body. Sometimes she prepares more than one nest while awaiting the arrival of the young. Apparently she cannot tell when the young are about to be born; the event may take place when she is out hunting for food. When it happens, she feeds the babies wherever she may be, then, one by one, takes them to the nest and covers them. The babies are born blind and deaf, usually four or five to a litter.

Because her movements may be observed, she visits the nest to feed her young only when necessary. Except when she is away searching for food, she stands watch near the nest. If an intruder, such as another rabbit or a squirrel, comes near the nest she will rush out and drive it away. A mother rabbit has even been known to attack predators when her babies were threatened. The young grow rapidly. In five or six days they can see and hear. By the time they are two weeks old, they can make short trips away from the nest. For a few days, they do not go far from the nest, but make their own hiding places and learn to eat plants. However, they return to the nest at night. Soon they drift away to seek their own territories.

The cottontail is seldom found in the forest, but prefers the fringes of meadows, brushlands, and especially piles of downed branches. During summer, it eats nearly anything green; in winter it subsists on woody foods. Since they live mainly in the lower elevations, there are few sight records from the three parks.

OCCURRENCE AND DISTRIBUTION:

Audubon Cottontail *(Sylvilagus audubonii)*

Sequoia–Kings Canyon: Rare. Recorded only in southern sector, Foothill Zone.

Yosemite: Not recorded.

Brush Rabbit *(Sylvilagus backmani)*

Sequoia–Kings Canyon: Uncommon. Recorded in chaparral belt in southern sector, Foothill Zone.

High Sierra Zone
Mid-Sierra Zone
Foothill Zone

Yosemite: Rare. Foothill Zone.

High Sierra Zone
Mid-Sierra Zone
Foothill Zone

The Predators

All the mammals in this group are near or at the top of the food chain. Only the cougar and bear can be described as being at the top. Several of the smaller varieties, such as the skunk and ringtail eat animals smaller than themselves, but they may be eaten by still larger animals.

Predators might be described as "control animals." When a prey species, such as the mouse, rabbit, or even the deer, becomes too abundant, it comes under heavy hunting pressure from this group. A rapid drop-off in the prey population normally follows. With less food available, this tends to gradually reduce the number of predators in the region, allowing the prey species to establish a more stable population.

By nature, predators try to avoid contact with man and are observed less frequently than most mammals. Most are active at night.

Black Bear

Ursus americanus

There is little doubt that a bear is one of the most sought after attractions in the parks. Even the General Sherman Tree in Sequoia and Yosemite Falls, famous as they are, temporarily take a back seat when a bear wanders into the scene. If it should be a mother bear with cubs, everything else is forgotten for the moment, while the cubs become the center of attention. Nor does interest seem to lessen until they drift away into the forest.

Although usually referred to as the black bear, it may be found in a variety of colors ranging from black to brown, yellowish or reddish-cinnamon. Even members of the same family may be of different colors. The bear is a remarkably clean animal, and bathes frequently during the warm, summer months. It takes mud or dust baths to rid itself of insect pests, but it doesn't allow the dirt to remain in its fur for long. Except when it is shedding, it is a well groomed animal. Most adult bears weigh from 200–300 pounds, although one old male at Yosemite weighed in at 590 pounds!

A grown bear is mostly solitary in its habits. Seldom are two seen together, except at mating time in early summer. Even this period of companionship lasts less than a month. After mating, the male goes his way, more concerned about finding food and a comfortable place to sleep than any further association with his short-term mate. In early fall, the female begins her search for a suitable winter den in which to give birth to her cubs. She may choose a hollow in a tree or fallen log, or she may prefer a cave under a rocky ledge. To make it warmer, she often uses leaves, pine needles or rotting wood for her bed. The arrival of cold weather finds her comfortably situated, awaiting the arrival of her cubs. During this time she does not hibernate in the true sense, but simply enters a deep sleep.

In January, the cubs are born. Normally there are two, but she may have only one or as many as four. At birth, the cub is about nine inches long and weighs eight to ten ounces, is blind and has neither hair nor teeth. Instinctively he nuzzles his mother until he finds his first drink of milk. It is essential that he take care of himself at this early age, as his mother is often too drowsy to pay much attention to him.

When spring arrives, the cubs will each weigh about four pounds, and it is time to leave the den. Their mother takes them out to begin their training. This will last for more than a year, during which time they will learn where to find food and how to protect themselves if danger threatens. They are given this training with affection, but with severe discipline. She is careful to see that they obey at all times. Obedience is vital, as a young cub could become a meal for a coyote if caught away from the protection of its mother. Even a wandering old male bear will sometimes kill and eat a cub if he should find it alone. At the first suggestion of danger, the mother sends the cubs up a tree. Despite their roly-poly appearance, they can climb almost as readily as a squirrel.

With the arrival of summer, the cubs have the time of their lives. They eat more or less continuously, roll and tumble on the meadow grass, and have wrestling and boxing contests. Frequently their mother sends them up a tree while she does other things where their presence might be a problem. At such times, the cubs drape themselves on branches and sleep away the hours until she returns.

Fall finds the cubs still with their mother, but now they are several inches taller, and weigh thirty-five to forty-five pounds. By November they are usually back in the den, furry and fat, and ready for the long winter season.

The second summer is spent with their mother, but now they are old enough to take care of themselves. By fall they leave and are on their own. Often the two cubs stay together for their first winter alone, but soon they drift apart.

For a bear, food is nearly anything edible, although it prefers meat. It wanders through the forest tearing open rotten logs or old stumps, searching for insect larvae. The meadows furnish a wide variety of food. It likes grass and clover, especially in the spring months when both are young and tender. It likes lily, wild onion and brodiaea bulbs, and it is fond of fruit, particularly manzanita, service berry, elderberry, and wild cherry. Chipmunks, ground squirrels, marmots, pocket gophers, and mice all are a part of its diet. Never choosy, it eats carpenter ants, crickets, grasshoppers, fish of any kind, and even carrion. In the fall, it gorges on acorns, and may often be seen searching for them beneath the oak trees.

Always remember that the bear in the forest is not tame simply because it happens to be in a national park. It is always potentially dangerous, and offering it food is taking a serious risk—to limb, if not to life. The bear poses no threat if left alone, and should be watched from a respectable distance. Follow the advice of an old-time ranger who said: "Never get closer to a bear than thirty feet—whether you're running toward him, or he's running toward you!"

OCCURRENCE AND DISTRIBUTION:

Sequoia–Kings Canyon: Common. Mid-Sierra Zone into High Sierra Zone. Occasionally visits the Foothill Zone in winter.

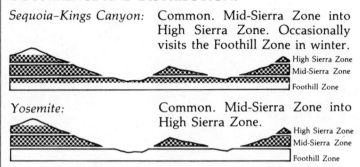

Yosemite: Common. Mid-Sierra Zone into High Sierra Zone.

Ringtail

(Civet Cat, Bassariscus)
Bassariscus astutus

The ringtail is known by many names, depending on where it lives. It is called "bassariscus," "cacomistle," "civet cat," "coon cat," "ring-tailed cat," "band-tailed cat," or "miner's cat." The interesting thing about the names, of course, is that it isn't a cat at all, but a cousin of the racoon and the black bear. Its pointed nose gives it a fox-like appearance, but the prominent black rings on its long tail resemble those of the raccoon (although, unlike the raccoon's rings, they do not go entirely around the tail). Its scientific name, *Bassariscus astutus*, means "clever little fox" and it certainly deserves the title.

This shy animal is seldom seen, as it hunts mainly at night. Occasionally it sun bathes, but only when it is not likely to be seen. It spends most of the daylight hours asleep in some well-hidden spot, in a hollow tree, under a rocky ledge, or in a rock slide. Unlike most mammals, it seems to enjoy associating with others of its kind, sharing the same shelter without friction.

The ringtail is one of nature's important "control" animals, as it kills and eats large numbers of small rodents that otherwise could become too abundant. It is especially fond of woodrats and deer mice, but it also helps hold down the chipmunk and ground squirrel populations. Nor does it hunt only on the ground. It is an excellent climber and often takes to the bushes and trees at night hoping to surprise some sleeping bird or rob a nest of the young. Its large, dark eyes are especially adapted for seeing at night, giving it a valuable advantage. Brush-dwelling birds, such as towhees and sparrows, are often a part of its diet. When hunting, it covers an extensive area, but travels in an erratic fashion, as it may cross and recross one small sector several times. In its wanderings, it finds and eats insects of various kinds. Though it prefers an animal diet, it enjoys wild fruits, such as manzanita berries.

In preparation for the arrival of her young, the mother may use the shelter she has been occupying, or she may look for better quarters. A hollow tree or dark hole beneath a rocky ledge may be selected. This latter location is especially desirable if the former occupant was a woodrat and left the usual debris pile of sticks. Prior to giving birth of her young, she drives the male away. He will return later to help her feed and care for them.

The young are born in May or early June. There are usually three or four kittens in a litter, and they arrive completely unable to help care for themselves. They are born blind, without teeth, and with their ears closed. However, within a few days they change rapidly. By the time they are three to four weeks old, their parents commence feeding them some meat. Soon afterward their eyes open, and they begin the task of learning how to walk. By the time they are two months old, they are taken on nightly trips with their parents, at which time they are taught how to hunt. At four months, they are entirely weaned. Now it is time for them to leave the den and make their own living.

If the young ringtails have learned their lessons well, they will survive to adulthood. They must be constantly on the alert, for the great horned owl and bobcat are ever present threats. Occasionally, a young ringtail falls prey to a rattlesnake. The ringtail has three primary means of defense: its agility, its alertness, and the use of an anal musk gland that secretes a sweet-smelling substance obnoxious to its enemies.

There are many records of ringtails taking up residence in buildings, especially in the attics of houses. One was once found nesting in a large chest of drawers in a spare bedroom. It came and went on its nightly hunts so silently that the family living in the house wasn't aware of its presence.

OCCURRENCE AND DISTRIBUTION:

Sequoia–Kings Canyon: Common. Foothill Zone into the Mid-Sierra Zone.

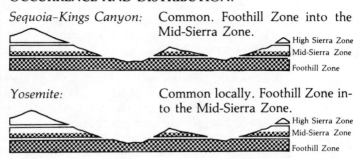

High Sierra Zone
Mid-Sierra Zone
Foothill Zone

Yosemite: Common locally. Foothill Zone into the Mid-Sierra Zone.

High Sierra Zone
Mid-Sierra Zone
Foothill Zone

Raccoon
Procyon lotor

A churring, bird-like call coming out of the darkness of night may be just what it sounds like—a bird disturbed in its sleep and giving voice to its uneasiness. It may be also a family of raccoons out for its nightly hunt, the mother leading the way, closely followed by four or five young, all talking among themselves. Most mammals are relatively quiet unless frightened or angry, but raccoons are an exception. They will growl when angry, but the bird-like churring is their usual means of communication.

Raccoons live in the lower valleys and seldom venture above the middle elevations. Their dens are usually in holes in trees or hollow logs, but they may also inhabit old deserted buildings. Several raccoons may occupy the same quarters, but in most instances they will be members of the same family. They prefer to live in wooded areas, near stream courses or lakes, for areas like these provide much of their food. This often puts them in close proximity with man, as he too likes to live near water. This close contact with man doesn't seem to bother the raccoons, and they often visit campgrounds or houses in search of food. While normally out at night, they become so accustomed to visitors that they occasionally come out in the daytime.

One habit of the raccoon that has long been a source of speculation is why it washes its food before eating. Some biologists have suggested that washing makes the food easier to swallow. Others maintain that the raccoon really doesn't wash the food; it just dunks it in water because it enjoys the sensation. Others maintain it lacks enough saliva to moisten the food thoroughly before it is swallowed. Whatever the reason, it does wash its food whenever it can, giving rise to the name of "lotor," meaning "one who washes."

The raccoon is a surly animal and frequently displays a short temper. Members of the same family often quarrel and even fight viciously. When members of different families get together, there is almost certain to be a pitched battle with several animals involved in one clawing, biting, snarling mass. An opponent's tail is often the target of well-aimed bites. In spite of quarrels, several may band together in the winter, apparently for warmth. The raccoon does not hibernate, but simply drops into a heavy sleep.

While the male raccoon is polygamous, the female won't mate with just any male. Her mate must be acceptable before

she will have anything to do with him. Once she has made up her mind, she refuses to have any kind of a relationship with another male that season. Mating takes place during the winter months, and the young are born about nine weeks later. The male takes no part in raising the family, leaving those duties to the mother.

After finding a good place to give birth to her family—usually a hollow tree if one can be found—she settles down to the task of raising the four or five young. When first born, the young raccoons are unable to see, but their eyes open about the third week. They grow rapidly, and within two months, the mother begins weaning them. Now she will take them with her on short trips near their home. While traveling she leads the way with the cubs usually in single file behind, churring as they go.

Her first task is to teach them to care for themselves. She leads them to a stream or lake where they can explore the shallow water and shoreline for frogs and water insects. They learn how to catch fish. Their method is to trap slow-moving fish in shallow water; or with their sensitive fingers, feel under the overhanging vegetation along the stream bank for any careless fish that might be resting there. Old logs are investigated to obtain the large white grubs that live in the rotting wood. They also learn to catch grasshoppers, and the eggs of ground-dwelling birds are eagerly sought and eaten. If they should find a mouse's nest, the young mice are quickly gobbled up. In late summer and early fall, they enjoy wild grapes, manzanita berries, elderberries and other fruit. Most, but not all, of these foods are taken to the nearest water and washed—or dunked—before being eaten.

During the training period, the mother raccoon must be constantly alert to protect her young family. Normally they are safe if she is near, as she is a brave and fearless defender, and few enemies care to face her. An unprotected cub would have little chance to survive if it should happen to meet a hungry bobcat or cougar. The mother stays with her family through the first winter. After that they go their separate ways.

OCCURRENCE AND DISTRIBUTION:

Sequoia–Kings Canyon: Common locally. Foothill Zone into Mid-Sierra Zone.

High Sierra Zone
Mid-Sierra Zone
Foothill Zone

Yosemite: Abundant locally. Foothill Zone into Mid-Sierra Zone.

High Sierra Zone
Mid-Sierra Zone
Foothill Zone

Marten

(Pine Marten)
Martes americana

If they were able to vote, the members of the squirrel family would certainly place the marten right at the top of their list of dangerous enemies. Not only can it run faster than a squirrel, climb trees and jump from one to another quite as easily, but the marten is almost tireless in its hunting. Unless the squirrel can squeeze into a hole that is too small for its pursuer, its minutes are numbered.

As a hunter, the marten has few equals. Unlike most members of the weasel family, it hunts mostly in the tree tops, jumping from one tree to another, and often covering distances of a mile or more before coming to the ground. On the ground, it may cover as much as ten miles in a single night. Any likely place that might harbor a squirrel, a bird or bird nest, is carefully investigated. Because it hunts both night and day, it has a wide variety of prey. Although it seems to prefer tree squirrels, it feeds regularly on mantled-ground squirrels, chipmunks, young marmots, rabbits, woodrats, and mice. It eats birds, including such large species as the dusky grouse and quail. It eats frogs, some species of reptile, insects, and occasionally ripe berries. If hunting is poor, it will even eat carrion. Because all these foods are normally in good supply, the marten seldom goes hungry. Even though it finds an abundance of food, it kills only what it needs, burying any excess for future use.

Its search for food frequently brings it into contact with man. Although it is normally afraid of people, its intense curiosity will sometimes drive it into a campground to see what campers are doing. Unattended food may be taken from the tables and carried into the tree tops. Martens have been known to investigate houses and inviting garbage cans.

The marten is an exceptionally agile and graceful animal. It bounds rather than runs, and is on the move much of its waking hours. It sleeps whenever it feels the need, whether day or night. Occasionally it relaxes a bit and takes a sun bath, but this is not a regular activity. While the beauty of its fur is admired, its temperament is not attractive. Short-tempered and vicious, it will attack even members of its own family. Only at mating time will it accept any companionship. The male will tolerate the female then, but

becomes a thing of fury should a competing male appear.

The mating season begins in July and extends into August, and the male goes his own way soon after. The gestation period is somewhat unusual, in that for an interval of several weeks, the development of the embryo is suspended. However, after about nine months, the young arrive, usually in April.

The mother usually selects a hollow tree or dead snag for her family, and lines the nest with grass or other soft materials. The new born young are blind and covered with fine hair. In about a month, their eyes open, and the fast-growing youngsters begin to abandon milk for meat. They grow to adult size and weight by midsummer and fall finds them living solitary lives.

The marten is accustomed to all sorts of temperatures, and can withstand the most rigorous winter. It does not hibernate, but is active throughout the cold months. During this time, hair grows on the soles of its feet, protecting them from the cold and enabling the animal to run across the snow without difficulty. Its hunting activities may be curtailed by heavy storms, but at such times it simply curls up in a warm shelter and waits for the weather to clear. If prey becomes too scarce in the higher elevations during the winter, it may move down into the middle-zone forests to obtain its prey.

With its great quickness and savage temper, there are few animals that care to challenge the marten. Should the need arise, it has a pair of musk glands that discharge a noxious-smelling fluid. This usually sends the challenger on its way. Its close cousin, the fisher, relishes marten meat, and the bobcat is believed to kill one occasionally. Then, of course, there is man. In many parts of the West, the marten's numbers are now greatly reduced. Large areas that once were heavily forested have been made unsuitable for them through lumbering. Trapping has accounted for many more. Fortunately, the marten's value is being finally recognized, and it is now totally protected in our national parks.

OCCURRENCE AND DISTRIBUTION:

Sequoia–Kings Canyon: Uncommon. High Sierra Zone.

High Sierra Zone
Mid-Sierra Zone
Foothill Zone

Yosemite: Common. High Sierra Zone.

High Sierra Zone
Mid-Sierra Zone
Foothill Zone

114

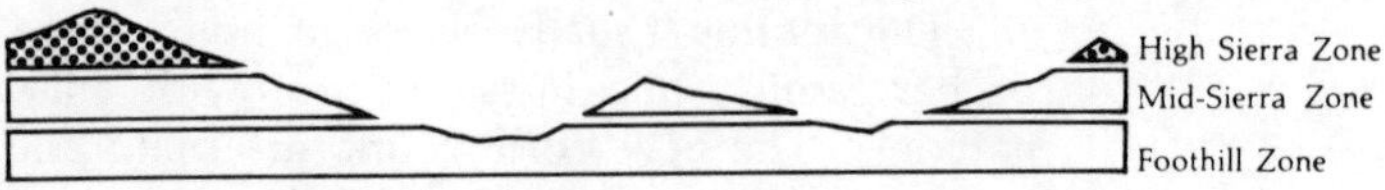

Fisher

(Fisher Cat, Black Cat)
Martes pennanti

This large, fox-sized, dark-furred member of the weasel family is known by several names, depending upon the section of the country where it is found. It is not a cat, but it is sometimes called "fisher cat" or "black cat." It is also known as "fisher marten." The Chippewa Indians had the most descriptive name for it. They called it "the-cho," which means "big marten," a name that recognizes its close relationship to its smaller cousin, the marten.

The fisher prefers the thick forest, especially if it is a bit damp or swampy. It swims well and occasionally crosses streams and even lakes. It is seldom seen by park visitors for it normally hunts at night, and its dark form is difficult to see. To make sight observations even more unlikely, it often ranges through the tree tops in its search for food. Extremely sure-footed and agile, it can travel faster through the trees than any other Sierran mammal, including the squirrel and the marten.

While its name suggests that it catches and eats fish, such is not the case. Occasionally it may enter the water to catch a diseased or dying fish, but it doesn't "go fishing." Instead it depends upon its hunting skills for food. It prefers meat, and any of the small animals is acceptable. The fisher runs with a bounding motion, covering about three to five feet in a leap. Such speed enables it to outrun rabbits. Raccoons and foxes frequently become prey. It is one of the few animals that can kill the well-armed porcupine without suffering any major damage from the sharp quills. The slow-moving porcupine has little chance against this enemy. The fisher simply flips porky over on its back and quickly attacks the unprotected stomach. Although some members of the weasel family are known to kill more than can be eaten, the fisher kills only what it needs, storing any surplus for the future. If meat becomes scarce, it will eat fruits and vegetables. At such times, it may descend to the middle forest zone or below, looking along the ridges for the most part.

Mating time for the fisher is sometime in April, after which the male immediately goes his way, leaving the family duties to the female. About eleven months later, in late March or early April, the young are born. When they first

arrive, the young are blind, a condition that lasts about seven weeks. When the babies are only about a week old, the mother leaves them for a few days while she goes away to mate again. Then she hurries back to feed her family. When they are about three months old, the young fishers are ready to leave the den and learn hunting skills from their mother. By fall, the family breaks up.

Fortunate is the person who has the rare privilege of seeing this elusive animal that has been described as having "a face of a weasel and the tail of a fox."

OCCURRENCE AND DISTRIBUTION:

Sequoia–Kings Canyon: Rare. High Sierra Zone into Mid-Sierra Zone.

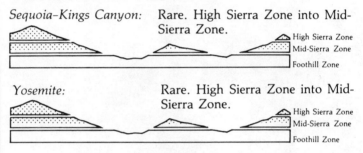

Yosemite: Rare. High Sierra Zone into Mid-Sierra Zone.

Weasel
Mustela spp.

Graceful, agile, intelligent, fearless, blood-thirsty, deadly—all these terms have been used to describe the weasel, and it deserves all of them. Seldom in nature is there found an animal capable of arousing admiration and anger all at the same time, but the weasel can and does.

For such a tiny creature, it controls events around it with sureness and success. As a hunter it has few equals. If faced with danger, it defends itself with great courage and skill, regardless of the size of its enemy. It is capable of adapting to almost any condition, whether it is from adverse weather or a direct confrontation with man.

You will often see weasels in a campground or around buildings. A female once raised her family inside a hollow log between the visitor cabins at Giant Forest in Sequoia, apparently completely unconcerned about the people walking within ten feet of her home. It shows great curiosity and investigates whatever seems of interest.

Its den is usually a hole beneath a tree or rock, in a hollow log, or it may take over the home of one of its victims. The den is made comfortable by lining the sleeping quarters with mouse fur, feathers or whatever else it finds to be desirable. It keeps the occupied part of the den clean of debris, and all droppings are taken outside. Often it sets aside one room for a toilet and one for garbage, and perhaps a third for storing surplus food.

Mating takes place in July or August, and the male immediately goes his own way. After partial development, the growth of the embryos is halted during the winter months. In March, the embryos begin to grow again, and birth takes place in April or May. The number of young varies from one to as many as ten. When first born they are almost naked, pink-skinned, toothless and blind. About five weeks later, their eyes open and they are ready for weaning and for their first hunting lessons. Summer's end finds them fully grown, the young males much larger than their mother, and ready to start life on their own.

The weasel seems to prefer to hunt at night. It may cover several miles in its search for food, but it goes no more than a few hundred yards from its den. It hunts in random fashion, crossing and recrossing its own trail several times. Perhaps this is because it hunts by scent rather than by sight.

Mice are an important part of its diet. In addition it eats woodrats, squirrels, chipmunks, mantled ground squirrels, pocket gophers, pikas, birds, and occasionally frogs and lizards. Although it prefers meat, it will eat certain insects. It requires an enormous quantity of food to supply the energy it burns, and it has been estimated that the longtail weasel kills about 1,300 mice each year. If hunting is good, it will eat half its own weight every twenty-four hours. With such a voracious appetite, you might expect that the weasel would quickly destroy the small animal life in its hunting territory, but it seldom does. Nor does it seem to frighten them away. Chipmunks may live near its den, and birds build nests and raise young in the surrounding forest. Although the weasel can climb to tree nests, it seldom does, preferring to hunt near or on the ground.

The number of weasels in any area is effectively determined by the abundance of small game. If a weasel destroys too many, its own young will find it difficult to survive. On the other hand, liked or hated, it serves as an effective control of small animal populations, keeping them at levels compatible with their food supply.

OCCURRENCE AND DISTRIBUTION:

Longtail Weasel *(Mustela frenata)*

Sequoia–Kings Canyon: Uncommon. High Sierra Zone into Mid-Sierra Zone

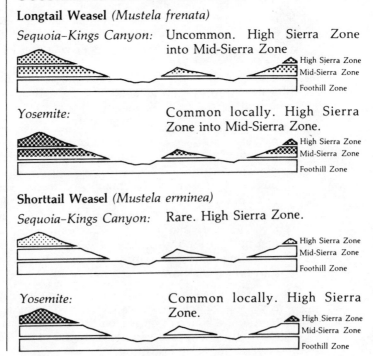

Yosemite: Common locally. High Sierra Zone into Mid-Sierra Zone.

Shorttail Weasel *(Mustela erminea)*

Sequoia–Kings Canyon: Rare. High Sierra Zone.

Yosemite: Common locally. High Sierra Zone.

Mink
Mustela vison

"Hunts like a weasel, swims like an otter" is an appropriate description of the mink. As a hunter, it rivals its cousin the weasel in its relentless pursuit of its prey. Like another cousin, the otter, it is an expert swimmer and can overtake a fish.

The mink may spend its days in a number of living situations, but it prefers to live near lakes and streams where it spends a lot of time in the water. Its den may be beneath the roots of a tree, along a stream, or in a hole in the bank with a well defined trail leading to the water. It may go on hunting trips that take it several miles from home, sleeping in the burrow of one of its victims. It returns home only when it has almost exhausted the food supply in the area.

The mink establishes a relatively small territory. The female may require less than one square mile; the male a much larger area. However, during the winter when snow is on the ground, it generally stays in its den, sleeping much of the time. It does not hibernate, but is inactive except for occasional hunting trips.

The mink eats a variety of food. Living as it does around water, it is very fond of trout. It eats crayfish and frogs when it can find them. Like the weasel, it kills and eats great numbers of meadow mice and other small rodents. The cottontail is a favorite prey. It hunts muskrats, and may destroy an entire colony before searching for other food. It catches wild ducks around the marshes and streams, especially those weak or injured, and any smaller birdlife it can surprise. As it does not climb, perching birds have little reason to fear it. It is a remarkably strong animal for its size, and will often carry heavy prey back to its den. Sometimes its supply of uneaten food in its bedroom is quite extensive.

The mating season usually occurs in February. The male travels over a considerable territory at this time hunting a mate. During his prowling, he may have several affairs before he settles down with the female of his choice. For the next several months, he is a devoted member of the family. The young are born about six weeks after mating, although there is some evidence that this period may be longer, as it is with some of the mink's cousins. The young number from four to eight, and are blind at birth. They are able to see when about five weeks old, at which time the mother weans them and teaches them to eat meat. When they are strong enough to travel, the parents begin training them to hunt. This often takes the family from its permanent den for several days. They may seek another hunting area before returning home. When the summer nears its end, the family breaks up and goes their separate ways. This is necessary in order to give each animal time to find its own territory and establish a den before winter arrives.

The mink has few enemies. The bobcat and fox sometimes catch one, and occasionally the great-horned owl surprises one at night. Because it is so quick, the mink is usually able to elude its attacker. It possesses a very strong, evil-smelling scent that it can discharge if needed. There is some doubt that this affords much protection as is true with the skunk. If attacked, it puts up a fierce battle, hissing and spitting with rage. Often this is sufficient to send the attacker on its way.

For many years, man has been one of the mink's most dangerous enemies, trapping large numbers for the fine fur.

OCCURRENCE AND DISTRIBUTION:

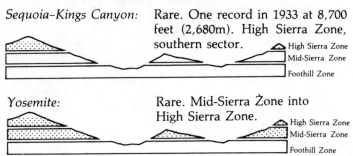

Sequoia–Kings Canyon: Rare. One record in 1933 at 8,700 feet (2,680m). High Sierra Zone, southern sector.

High Sierra Zone
Mid-Sierra Zone
Foothill Zone

Yosemite: Rare. Mid-Sierra Zone into High Sierra Zone.

High Sierra Zone
Mid-Sierra Zone
Foothill Zone

Wolverine

(Skunk-bear, Glutton)
Gulo gulo

Few animals have been the subject of so many stories, fact and fancy, as this powerful member of the weasel family. Legends fill the literature with tales of its strength, ferocity, cunning, destructiveness, and malicious meanness. Some say it is one of Satan's own creations, having no redeeming values, possessed of diabolical cleverness, enabling it to even outwit man. Along the way it has also accumulated several descriptive names, such as "skunk-bear" and "glutton."

That the wolverine is a courageous fighter is well established. It will not hesitate to attack any animal larger than itself when food is concerned. There are records of it actually driving a grown bear and cougar away from food it wants. With its powerful jaws, long claws, great quickness and bad temper, it presents a menacing figure to other forest dwellers and none care to challenge it.

Its prey includes some of the larger animals, and it will attack and kill a deer hampered by deep snow. It will kill and eat almost any animal it can overpower. Its big body requires lots of food to keep it active, and it destroys large numbers of smaller animals, such as marmots, rabbits, squirrels, woodrats, and any of the larger birds it can catch. It doesn't waste any of what it kills. If there is too much for one meal, it usually just waits around until its stomach can hold some more and then eats what is left. Any food not eaten is cached for a later meal. Although it prefers live prey, it will eat carrion. It uses its great strength to rip open rotting logs and to overturn rocks that may hide small animal burrows. it doesn't like to dig for prey, although its long claws are effective in moving dirt. Despite its cunning, it sometimes fails to display caution when attacking a porcupine, and there are known instances where the wolverine has been found dead with many quills imbedded in the body. Apparently the quills had reached some vital organs, causing death.

The wolverine is a loner and has little to do with others of his kind. It is territorial. This may be because there is too much competition for food, or perhaps it simply cannot get along with others. The male makes an exception to this in late winter. In February or March he searches for a mate. After finding one, the courtship is brief. Soon the male goes

its way, while the female returns to her solitary life.

Young wolverines are born in June. There are usually two or three in a litter, although there may be as many as five. The den is normally located in a part of the forest where dense foliage covers the ground, in a hollow tree, or, in the higher elevations, under an overhanging rock. When first born, the young are pale brown. This rapidly changes into the dark coat they will have when fully grown. They grow rapidly, and by late fall or early winter, they are on their own.

The wolverine ranges over a large territory, and may travel several miles in a single night. It does not hibernate and is out in all sorts of weather. Stiff hairs on the soles of its feet enable it to move about easily on snow. It spends the winter in the higher forests and on the open slopes near forest line. Park rangers on high-country ski patrol have found wolverine tracks on several occasions.

Except for the danger from man, the wolverine is seldom concerned for his safety. Its fierce manner alone is usually sufficient to send any potential attacker on its way. Although possessing a strong, vile smelling musk it can eject if necessary, the wolverine seldom uses this defense weapon.

Given their solitary habits and large territory, it is doubtful that wolverines have ever been numerous in the Sierra. However, fortunate and sharp-eyed high-country hikers may occasionally see one.

OCCURRENCE AND DISTRIBUTION:

Sequoia–Kings Canyon: Rare. High Sierra Zone into Mid-Sierra Zone.

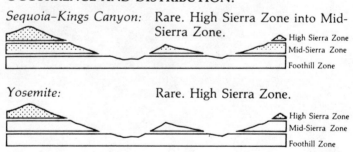

Yosemite: Rare. High Sierra Zone.

Badger
Taxidea taxus

The badger has a wide altitudinal range, and is as much at home in the high country of the Sierra as in the valleys and deserts near sea level. The availability of ground-dwelling rodents determines where it will live. It prefers open meadows at almost any elevation. In such situations, mice, ground squirrels and pocket gophers are found in abundance. Unlike other members of the weasel family, the badger can neither run down his prey, nor climb trees in search of food. Thus, it is obliged to catch them in their burrows, and this it can do exceptionally well. It is blessed with an unusually sensitive nose, and can easily detect when a burrow is occupied. Then follows a contest with the occupant. The badger has short, powerful legs equipped with long claws specially designed for digging. Quickly it rips open the burrow. If the occupant has been prudent and constructed one or more exits, it will likely escape. If it hasn't, it is quickly cornered and killed. Most ground squirrels, mice, and other rodents dig relatively shallow burrows, which makes them easy prey for this skillful digger.

The ability to dig a hole in a matter of seconds gives the badger a good defense. When cornered it can dig itself quickly out of sight if the area is not rocky. Few animals will actually attack a badger. While it weighs only about ten to fifteen pounds, it is a fierce fighter, knows no fear, and always gives a good account of itself. Its powerful muscles, long hair and extremely tough hide enable it to survive where a less hardy animal would perish. Dogs find that cornering a badger is not difficult, but killing one is a dangerous business. When angry, it gives loud hisses as a warning. If the attacker doesn't take the hint, the badger may emit a strong odor from its musk glands. If all else fails, it is prepared to do battle. Man is the only enemy the badger cannot defend itself against.

The badger mates in autumn or early winter, depending somewhat upon the weather and the elevation where it lives. To prepare for the arrival of her young, the female digs a burrow deep underground, ending in a long tunnel with an enlarged room at the end. Here she prepares a nest of dry grass. During the cold months that follow, she sleeps much of the time, but does not hibernate. To stay warm, she closes off the burrow with loose dirt for protection against winter snow and wind. During this period of inactivity, the embryos stop growing for at least two months. They will begin growing again when spring is near. The young are born in May or June. They may range in number from one to seven; normally there are three.

Like other musk bearers, the young badgers are born blind and helpless. About four to five weeks later, the eyes open, and they become quite active. When they are about half grown, the mother weans them. She will continue to feed them, however, until they have developed hunting skills and are ready to take care of themselves. In late summer, the young badgers go their respective ways, and the mother prepares to mate again.

The badger is an important control on the numbers of rodents in its territory. When rodents become too numerous, the badger finds hunting very good. Having a good appetite, it soon helps to reduce the numbers to a more normal level. The badger contributes to the wildlife scene in still another way. It often changes its home and digs a new burrow. The old one is soon taken over by some smaller animal. Foxes and coyotes find that enlarging a deserted badger den is much easier than digging a new one.

OCCURRENCE AND DISTRIBUTION:

Sequoia–Kings Canyon: Rare. Foothill Zone to around 10,000 feet (3,000m) in the High Sierra Zone.

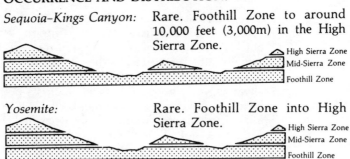

Yosemite: Rare. Foothill Zone into High Sierra Zone.

Spotted Skunk

(Hydrophobia Cat, Civet Cat)
Spilogale putorius

The spotted skunk is certainly the prettiest, smallest and most agile of all the skunks. It is also the most likely to appear where least expected. It is not particularly afraid of man, and may come into a campground or investigate cabins, even when occupied by visitors. There are numerous records of its taking up residence in the attics of homes. One was even seen walking serenely down a hallway in a park employee's home, entirely unconcerned over the consternation that arose when it met the occupant. It is very curious and investigates all sorts of places. A garbage can, full or empty, is a great attraction. It quickly learns how to raise the hinged lid of a garbage can and slip inside, but it never seems to learn how to get out! It sits inside, crying out occasionally, until someone sets it free, an operation usually carried out with considerable caution!

It is a master at the art of self-defense. As do other skunks, it has scent glands, but it has a different warning technique when threatened. Facing the potential attacker, it stamps its front feet vigorously on the ground. If this fails to achieve the desired result, it may prepare to spray its scent in the usual fashion, or it may improve on that by doing a "hand stand" on its front feet, waving its hind quarters in the air. Faced with this forbidding spectacle, the intruder usually goes on about its business. Normally the spotted skunk is mild-tempered and gentle, and uses its powerful scent only when it is cornered. If given the chance, it will back away peacefully from a difficult situation.

It is an excellent hunter. Starting out in the early evening, it visits the most likely spots for mice. This takes it to the meadows and brushy areas, where it exercises its agility and hunting skills by catching meadow mice and white-footed mice. It has little difficulty catching these little rodents, and they constitute an important source of food. In turn, the skunk helps control the mouse population. It also preys on woodrats, pocket gophers, and chipmunks, and it will even attack rabbits and hares larger than itself. It often hunts along streams and small ponds for frogs and salamanders. Lizards and small snakes are eaten when they can be found. It will even eat carrion if other food is unavailable.

In its wanderings, it frequently finds the nests of ground-dwelling birds; the eggs and nestlings make excellent meals. There is little doubt that the quail population is affected by these hunting activities. It is also fond of insects. During the summer and fall, grasshoppers, crickets, and larvae of various kinds comprise a large part of its diet. Although it prefers a meat diet, it eats quantities of ripe fruits and competes with other animals for mushrooms.

Almost any kind of a shelter serves as a home. A rocky crevice is a favorite location, especially a narrow one that extends several feet into the rock wall. This affords almost perfect protection from its enemies. It may also use an abandoned burrow of a marmot or badger, or it may settle for a hollow log or stump.

Finding a suitable home by the time fall arrives is especially important to the female. It will serve as her winter abode, and it is here her babies will be born. Breeding takes place in late winter, and the young make their appearance in early spring. Usually there are no more than four to a litter. When first born, the newborn skunk is blind, deaf and toothless. It does have one ability—it can emit a loud squeal if disturbed. It cries for food when hungry, and is able to see and hear by the time five weeks have passed. It is also able to walk, although a bit clumsily. At the age of five months, it is as big as its mother, and has learned much of what it will need to survive alone.

Unfortunately, the spotted skunk has gained a reputation as a bearer of hydrophobia, or rabies. Throughout many parts of the West, it is believed the animal carries this dread disease, and that it goes around biting people without provocation. This is not true. Studies do show that the bites from skunks of all kinds produce more cases of rabies than do the bites of any other wild animal. However, the spotted skunk is responsible for only about one percent of all rabies cases reported. In spite of this, many people still refer to it as the "hydrophobia cat," or simply "phoby cat."

OCCURRENCE AND DISTRIBUTION:

Sequoia–Kings Canyon and Yosemite: Common locally. Foothill Zone and Mid-Sierra Zone.

High Sierra Zone
Mid-Sierra Zone
Foothill Zone

Striped Skunk

Mephitis mephitis

The skunk is highly respected by other animals, including man. This respect does not come about because of the way it lives, but because of what it is able to do. Of all the musk-producing mammals of the Sierra, the scent possessed by the skunk is without doubt the most nauseating and ill-smelling of all. Add to that the fact that the skunk's delivery system is highly efficient, and it is easy to see why it has far fewer problems staying alive than most of its neighbors.

Although it doesn't discharge its scent without a good reason, it is always ready to do so when necessary. If it is threatened, it will first give a pointed warning by facing its enemy and raising its plumed tail above its back. If this doesn't cause the enemy to reconsider, the skunk may stamp its front feet vigorously. It may even growl or hiss. This constitutes a final warning. If not heeded, the skunk turns like a flash, presenting both ends of its body toward the intruder, at the same time discharging a fine spray from the musk glands. The discharge is accurate up to about ten feet with predictable results. The strong odor is very difficult to remove, whether from fur or clothing.

The skunk is a leisurely animal; never seeming to be in a hurry. It often finds itself away from its home after a night spent hunting. This poses no problem, as it just finds any convenient den or hollow log and uses it as a hiding place for the day. If the den is already occupied, it is perfectly all right; the skunk just goes to sleep.

It prefers to live in brushy areas, or where meadow and forest meet. Its home is often the deserted burrow of a fox, a marmot, or a badger. While it doesn't like to dig, it remodels the old burrow a bit, perhaps even adding a tunnel or two. Several feet from the entrance it makes its bedroom, if one isn't already there. Dead leaves and grass are brought in to make its sleeping quarters comfortable and warm. The skunk uses this den throughout the year and, being a clean animal, keeps it free of litter. When winter arrives, it prepares for cold weather by plugging the entrance to the den with leaves or other debris. Then it curls up in the bedroom to sleep away the days until warmer weather returns. The length of its sleep depends upon the temperature outside. Although it is inactive during this time, it does not hibernate. It simply becomes drowsy and can awaken very quickly if the need arises. Often its den offers a convenient place for other skunks to spend the winter, and their presence is accepted without any trouble.

The female mates in late winter or early spring. About eight weeks elapse before the young are born. There are usually three to eight of them, and they are born blind, without teeth, and nearly hairless. Growth is rapid, and at three weeks they are fully furred and able to see. The mother weans them at about two months. By this time they are big enough to accompany her on hunting trips away from the den. Insects are an important part of the diet, especially grasshoppers, crickets and various kinds of larvae. Berries are eaten also, and they soon learn how to catch mice. The young skunks also learn how to kill bees by stamping on them as they emerge from their nest. Eggs and nestlings of ground birds, such as quail and junco, are uncovered and eaten. Later in the year, as the young skunks become more adult in size, they may catch an occasional gopher, chipmunk or ground squirrel. If food should become scarce, even carrion is eaten.

Although usually well protected by its strong scent, there are times when the skunk faces real danger. When food for the larger predators is scarce, the cougar, bobcat, coyote, badger, and horned owl will attack and eat a skunk, despite its nauseating odor. But man remains its gravest enemy. Although not hunted or trapped in the parks, it is menaced by cars whenever it crosses a road at night. Too often it fails to escape.

OCCURRENCE AND DISTRIBUTION:

Sequoia–Kings Canyon: Common locally. Foothill Zone into lower Mid-Sierra Zone.

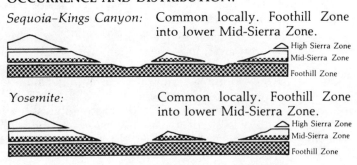

High Sierra Zone
Mid-Sierra Zone
Foothill Zone

Yosemite: Common locally. Foothill Zone into lower Mid-Sierra Zone.

High Sierra Zone
Mid-Sierra Zone
Foothill Zone

River
Otter

Lustra canadensis

If playfulness is any indication of freedom from anxieties and fears, the otter must live a relatively serene and carefree life. Seldom in nature will you find an animal that remains playful when it is fully grown, but the otter does. It revels in swimming, and a sloping bank above a stream or lake is an invitation it seems unable to resist. The slope soon becomes a slippery slide as the otter plunges into the water again and again. Sometimes it plays by itself; sometimes with friends. It has been known to spend several minutes tossing a flat rock into the water and diving after it. It doesn't restrict its love of sliding to the warm months, but becomes an animated toboggan on steep, snow-covered slopes. It has no problem keeping warm in cold weather as it has a layer of fat covering its body, and very short, thick underfur.

The otter is an expert swimmer and can stay under water for long periods of time without having to come up for air. Flaps close the nostrils and ears when it is under water. If it wishes, it can swim several hundred yards before coming to the surface. When submerged, the pulse slows markedly, allowing the animal to conserve oxygen. With its webbed feet and streamlined body, the otter can easily outswim most fishes, and it eats any kind it can find. Its diet is quite varied, with fresh-water snails and crayfish among the favorites. A muskrat family may furnish it with several meals. It relishes frogs, and is not adverse to eating snakes. If food becomes scarce, it will settle for tender water plants and various insects, both aquatic and dry-land species. Occasionally it adds a careless bird to its diet. However, it does most of its hunting in the water, for its hearing is poor and its legs are much too short to run down most land prey. Occasionally it will travel overland to other lakes and streams, but it seldom strays very far from water.

During the mating season, the male otter travels more than at any other time. As he roams, he leaves scent from his musk glands on tufts of grass to advertise his presence. This becomes quite useful in helping to locate a prospective mate, as females are attracted to the scent. Not being too selective, a male may have several mates during a season. After breed-

ing is over, the male usually spends most of the rest of his time alone. He has little to do with other males.

When the young are about to be born, the female prepares for the event by selecting a suitable burrow for her family. Often this is an abandoned bank burrow of a beaver or muskrat that can be easily renovated. She may choose a hollow log or the hollow base of a tree if not too far from water. The young otters—called pups—are usually born in April and number from one to five. Each baby is born with its eyes closed, a condition that does not change until it is about five weeks old. It cannot swim during its first few weeks. As soon as it can travel, the mother takes it to the water and patiently teaches it to swim and hunt. Once it has learned basic water skills, its development is rapid and it can soon take care of itself. During this period it plays a lot with the other pups in the litter and with its mother. Otter pups generally stay with their mother until they are almost a year old, and she is about to have another family. Then they must strike out on their own.

The otter has always lived in the lowland lakes and streams. Because there have been few records of otter in the higher parts of the Sierra, the presence of these animals today around the high lakes and streams is believed to have been caused by man's planting of trout in those waters. Any wild animal is likely to spread its territory into areas where food can be found in abundance. The stocking of lakes and streams in the Sierra for fishermen would certainly entice this expert fisherman into taking up residence.

OCCURRENCE AND DISTRIBUTION:

Sequoia–Kings Canyon: Not recorded in southern sector. One record in 1910 at Simpson Meadow, High Sierra Zone, in northern sector. Not reported since.

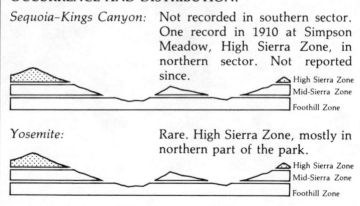

High Sierra Zone
Mid-Sierra Zone
Foothill Zone

Yosemite: Rare. High Sierra Zone, mostly in northern part of the park.

High Sierra Zone
Mid-Sierra Zone
Foothill Zone

Coyote
Canis latrans

If any animal can be said to typify the wild character of the West, it certainly would be the coyote. Its wild, high-pitched yodeling and barking that is heard coming from a brushy ridge late in the evening or at dawn is a sound that somehow seems to complete any mountain or desert scene.

The coyote is an animal of many personalities, depending upon who is describing it. To some ranchers it is a menace to their livestock; to others it is protected because of its value in destroying large numbers of rodents that are destructive to grasslands. Still others consider the coyote a very important member of the wildlife community. The coyote often lives close to man and even his cities, yet it is so wiley it escapes all but the experienced hunter or trapper. Although it is very wary of humans, it has a great curiosity; it may follow you apparently just to see what you are going to do. One coyote seemed fascinated by highway traffic, and was observed sitting a safe distance from the road, watching the cars go by. It is easy to see why, with all these traits, the coyote is admired and protected in some areas, but hated and condemned in others.

It is in its role as a hunter that the coyote makes its greatest contribution to the wildlife scene in the Parks. Wherever rodents become too numerous, there you will find the coyote looking for a meal. As most of its hunting is done at night, it preys primarily on those animals that are abroad at that time, such as mice, pocket gophers, woodrats, and rabbits. Other items on its diet include the chipmunk, chickaree, ground squirrel, marmot, frog, some small snakes, and any kind of bird it can catch. Insects, especially grasshoppers, are eaten with obvious relish. Though it is mainly a meat eater, it does eat considerable quantities of grass and berries in season. If food becomes scarce, it will settle for carrion of any kind. It may even risk attacking a porcupine.

Stories of the coyote killing large numbers of deer are greatly exaggerated. Occasionally, a coyote may find and kill a young fawn hidden in the brush, but such incidents are not common. There are instances when an old deer, weakened by disease or old age, falls prey to one or more coyotes. However, such happenings are beneficial to the deer population as only the strong survive to raise young. Occasionally a coyote will pick on a healthy deer that refuses to become a meal, and a wild chase follows, with the coyote scrambling to elude the enraged would-be victim.

Sometimes a male and female mate for several years, but usually a new mate is found as the occasion seems to warrant. The breeding season is in late winter and the young are born about two months later. To prepare for this event, the parents seek out a comfortable den. They may find what they want in a hollow log, in the base of a hollow tree, or in a cave. Or they may move into and remodel an old badger den. If the soil is easy to dig, they may decide to make their own den. Ordinarily a long tunnel is dug, with one or more side tunnels. The bedroom is situated at the end of the long tunnel and is usually free of any nesting materials.

While the female is awaiting the arrival of her pups, the male often brings food to her. When the pups arrive, the male moves out of the den for a few weeks, but during this time he hunts and brings food for the pups and his mate. The litter numbers from three to nine, depending somewhat upon the age of the mother, and possibly upon the abundance of food. Wobbly and awkward at birth, the pups develop rapidly and in a few days have grown enough to begin to take some meat to supplement their milk diet. The pups are dark gray at birth, making them difficult to see in the dim light of the den—important for their protection. However, when they are about ready to leave the den and begin their training, their color changes to a grayish-yellow that will help camouflage them in the sunlight. Both parents are involved in training the pups to hunt and care for themselves. It is during this period that one sometimes hears reports of "coyote packs"—actually a family group on a training operation. The young coyotes must leave the family before winter to establish their own territories. Sometimes this poses some difficult problems, as the region may already have a large number of coyotes, and no territories are available for the young animals. Failure to establish themselves before winter in an area where food can be found can be serious, even fatal, as they may starve before spring.

The adult coyote has few enemies in the wild, though it sometimes falls prey to a hungry cougar. The pup has more of a problem, as it may be killed by a bobcat, fisher, or wolverine, or occasionally by a golden eagle. Man is the most dangerous enemy of all. Over the West, he has killed thousands of coyotes by hunting and poisoning. In spite of man, it has adjusted to all problems of survival and is now found over most of the United States.

OCCURRENCE AND DISTRIBUTION:

Sequoia–Kings Canyon: Common generally. Foothill Zone
into High Sierra Zone.

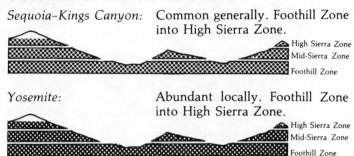

Yosemite: Abundant locally. Foothill Zone
into High Sierra Zone.

Red Fox
Vulpes fulva

The old riddle of "When is a red fox not a red fox?" can be answered in several ways. You might say "When it is a black fox"; or "When it is a silver fox"; or "When it is a cross fox." In every instance you would be correct.

The red fox, with its rich, reddish fur, black legs and feet, and its underparts and tip of tail white, is one of the most beautiful animals in the Sierra. However, in a litter of four pups, the female may have a group of young that hardly look related. One pup may be red; another may be black; another may have black fur, the hairs tipped with silvery white; while the fourth may be brownish-yellow with a broad black stripe running down the back and across the shoulders forming a cross. All these so-called red foxes have two markings in common—black legs and feet and a white-tipped tail. In the Sierra, the common color phase is the "cross fox." The red-coated fox is present, but in lesser numbers.

This is the largest and wiliest of the North American foxes. With its sharp eyes and sensitive ears, it is seldom surprised by an enemy. During its waking hours, it is constantly on the alert, watching for any movement and listening for any sound. While an adult in good health is not in much danger from other predators, it is occasionally killed by a coyote, bobcat or golden eagle. The young fox pups are constantly menaced by these animals. Many stories are told about men's contest of wits with the wily red fox. While man has won many such contests, he has also lost many, and the fox has continued to thrive and even to enlarge his territory.

While the red fox is considered to be one of the really rare animals of the Sierra, the lack of records may only mean that few observations have been made because of the animal's ability to escape detection, plus its choice of habitat. It likes the high elevation meadows and forests, and these are less visited by people than those of the middle elevations.

Living at higher elevations means the fox must be able to sustain itself during seasons when the temperatures are severe and the weather makes hunting difficult. Consequently its diet tends to be seasonal. During the summer, it depends upon small rodents such as mice, pocket gophers, pikas, chipmunks, ground squirrels, and marmots. It also eats ground-nesting birds and their eggs. The summer also furnishes an abundance of grasshoppers and beetles, and these are sometimes the most important food items for several days at a time. The late summer and early fall add such fruits as serviceberry, grape and elderberry to its meat diet. The arrival of winter means that most food must be captured and killed, as fruits and edible plants are gone. Some of the rodents are in hibernation while others stay under cover most of the winter, making hunting difficult. The depth of the snow at the higher elevations now becomes a major factor. During this time, the fox is largely dependent for food on the white-tail jackrabbit, the chickaree, and the flying squirrel. Mice are less easily caught, as most stay beneath the snow. Occasionally it can surprise and capture a blue grouse. If hunting gets really poor, it may risk trying to kill a porcupine. Trying to out-maneuver a porcupine sometimes ends with the porky going on about his business while the fox tries to survive with its face and mouth full of quills.

The red fox mates in winter, usually around February, and the pair stays together at least until the young are raised and ready to start out on their own. They often select an old, deserted fox or marmot den in which to raise their family. In a forested situation, the den is usually well hidden, but in an open meadow it is visible for some distance. Once the female is satisfied with the den, a nest is prepared for the family deep inside the burrow. About eight weeks after mating, the young are born. Their arrival is well timed, for now spring and warm weather are at hand, and small rodents are once more available. The pups range in number from four to nine, and are quite helpless at birth. However, by the time they are a month old, they are very active and growing at an astonishing rate. Both parents supply food for the family until the young foxes have learned the fundamentals of hunting. By fall or early winter, the young have drifted away from the den and have located their own shelters and hunting areas.

The red fox is an important control on rodent populations in the highlands. Without it and the wolverine, fisher, and weasel, there might be disastrous population explosions among the rodents that could seriously damage the plant cover in the grassy meadows and on the flower-laden slopes.

OCCURRENCE AND DISTRIBUTION:

Sequoia–Kings Canyon and Yosemite: Rare. High Sierra Zone.

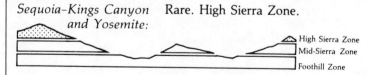

High Sierra Zone
Mid-Sierra Zone
Foothill Zone

Gray Fox

Urocyon cinereoargenteus

A grayish, rapidly moving shadow caught momentarily in the headlights of a car is the usual view one gets of this graceful animal. It is almost entirely nocturnal, but occasionally it is seen just about dusk, and in the early hours of dawn. At night, its eyes glow a vivid yellow-green in a beam of light, aiding in its identification. It is seldom observed during the daytime, although it is sometimes seen where brush is heavy. Often the only indication of its presence is a short, rather hoarse bark heard at night. It is shy, but it is also curious. If disturbed, it seldom runs very far before it takes cover. Then it watches to see what the intruder is going to do. It is adept at climbing trees, an ability not shared by other kinds of foxes. Almost any leaning tree seems to invite the gray fox to run up the trunk into the branches, where it sometimes curls up for a rest, or it may simply use the tree as an observation site. If pursued, it may climb a tree to escape.

This fox is one of the most important rodent hunters in the Sierra. It consumes large numbers of mice, pocket gophers, and woodrats. Any upsurge in the populations of these rodents brings on immediate hunting pressure by predators in the region, and the gray fox is one of the most successful of these. It also feeds on cottontails and ground squirrels. Birds, especially such ground-dwelling species as the quail, are captured occasionally. It is especially fond of bird eggs, and eats them shells and all. In season it feeds on grapes, wild cherries, elderberries, and manzanita berries. Tender grass is eaten in the spring, and is an important part of its diet. Sometimes man unwittingly provides the fox with a meal when his car kills a chipmunk or a squirrel. One fox was known to patrol a section of road each day during part of the summer to obtain meals.

The gray fox prefers the lower elevations where brushy slopes and valleys offer cover and protection, and where its favorite rodents are most abundant. Its home may be located in a variety of places, and when the ground is suitable, it may dig a burrow. Otherwise it may choose a large pile of loose rock, an overhanging ledge, a hollow log, or even a large hollow tree limb. Its nest is made of leaves, grass, bits of bark or any other material that might help to make a comfortable place to rest and sleep.

Mating takes place in late winter. It is sometimes accompanied by vicious fights between competing males for the attention of the female. These fights are seldom fatal, usually ending with one male deciding that the prize wasn't worth the effort. About two months after mating, two to five pups are born. Like the young of other wild dogs, they are helpless at birth, blind, and almost devoid of hair. The next few weeks are busy ones for the parents. The young soon grow enough for fresh meat to be added to their milk diet; fox pups consume a surprising number of small rodents. They spend some time outside the den playing with each other or with whatever seems interesting; for instance, bird feathers make great playthings. Soon they are big enough to be taken on hunting trips, and by the time late summer arrives, they have mastered survival skills and so drift away to establish their own homes.

The gray fox has many enemies, and the young are especially vulnerable. Coyotes, bobcats, fishers, and eagles find that a tender young pup makes an excellent meal. It is frequently weakened by parasites and diseases. With so many threats to its existence, the fox does not survive for many years, and it is an old animal that lives for more than five years.

In spite of large numbers of foxes destroyed each year by man, the gray fox has not only survived, but increased its range. While it prefers a warm climate, in the western part of the country it is slowly invading the colder regions of the north.

OCCURRENCE AND DISTRIBUTION:

Sequoia–Kings Canyon: Abundant locally, Foothill Zone.

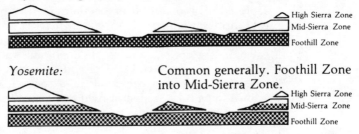

Yosemite: Common generally. Foothill Zone into Mid-Sierra Zone.

Cougar

(Mountain Lion)
Felis concolor

Without doubt, the mention that cougars are found over most of the Sierra has a greater effect upon the park visitor than the name of any other animal. Knowing that bears are in the forest arouses a bit of caution, but the thought of running into a cougar while on a hike often causes a change in hiking plans! This is unfortunate. The cougar wants nothing to do with anyone and offers no threat to your safety. Don't believe those stories which picture the big cat as being a dangerous, blood-thirsty creature just waiting for a chance to pounce upon an unsuspecting hiker.

The cougar is big by any standard, weighing up to 200 pounds and is often eight feet or more in length, including its tail. It is shy and alert, and you will be lucky to get even a fleeting look at it. The chances are it will know of your presence long before you have any idea it is near, and will simply fade away into the brush or the forest. It has a great curiosity and will sometimes follow an unsuspecting person at a respectable distance for several minutes unobserved before going on about its business.

The second misconception about the cougar is its eating habits. Many accounts have been written telling how the animal kills 200 or more deer each year, and that if allowed to live the cougar would completely destroy all the deer in a region. There is no doubt that when the deer population is high, the cougar does kill a great many; if the deer population is low, the number killed will be less. Studies show that under normal conditions, a cougar may kill as many as fifty to seventy-five deer a year. But it should be kept in mind that a high percentage of those killed are old deer, no longer alert and often diseased, or careless fawns. Thus the cougar serves to keep the deer herd strong, alert and healthy, preventing it from becoming too large and thus destructive to vegetation. Although the deer is the cougar's favorite food, there are other items on its diet. It gets an occasional bighorn in the highlands of the Sierra. Smaller mammals, such as rabbits, marmots, foxes, and raccoons are acceptable food. It may attack a porcupine, even though the big cat usually acquires numerous painful quills in the process. If success in hunting becomes a problem, it will even tackle a skunk.

The cougar seldom has an established den, except when raising a family. For that purpose the female may choose a shallow cave, a jumble of fallen logs, thick brush—almost anywhere that offers a good place to hide. Mating usually takes place in the winter, although it may occur at any time during the year. To advertise that he is looking for a mate, the male frequently scratches the ground, making bare spots. If the female finds these "courting" signs and his advances are acceptable, they pair off. Soon afterward the male leaves to resume his solitary life. His departure is essential, for male cats may kill and eat the kittens when they are born. The number of kittens range from one to five, with three the normal litter. At birth each kitten is blind, well furred with dark spots and a short, ringed tail. It retains the spots until it is about two months old when it gets its plain, tawny, adult coat. By this time, its diet includes fresh meat which the mother brings to the den. Soon it accompanies her and the other kittens on hunting trips. Patiently she teaches them the basic skills they will need as adults. The family remains together for about a year. By that time the young cougars are almost adult size and fully capable of caring for themselves.

Forced to shift for itself, the young cougar must find a territory of its own. This is often difficult as older and stronger cougars have usually established their own territories in regions where hunting is good. Sometimes these territories are large, covering several square miles. Thus it may be necessary for the newcomer to go several miles from where it was born before it can find an uncontested hunting territory.

The cougar has few enemies. Man and disease top the list. If undisturbed in the wilds it will likely live to a ripe old age before it is no longer able to catch enough prey to survive, or in a weakened condition it falls victim to disease. If it is a male, it may also be attacked and even killed by another male in a fight over territory. But the cougar's most dangerous and persistent enemy is man. He has hunted this big cat relentlessly ever since our country was settled, and only its skill in evading man has enabled the cougar to survive at all. Fortunately it is now protected against hunting in California. It is to be hoped that, as more people come to understand the cougar's place in the wildlife scene, they will give it more protection in areas outside the sanctuaries afforded by parks and other refuges.

OCCURRENCE AND DISTRIBUTION:

Sequoia–Kings Canyon: Uncommon. Foothill Zone and Mid-Sierra Zone.

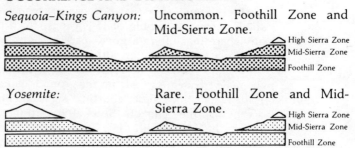

Yosemite: Rare. Foothill Zone and Mid-Sierra Zone.

Bobcat
Lynx rufus

The bobcat is a secretive animal, and its presence is seldom suspected. Daylight hours are mostly spent sunning itself on a secluded rock, lying under a bush in an area of dense undergrowth, or resting in a shallow cave digesting the food eaten the previous night. If an intruder should approach its resting place, it is almost a certainty the cat will know of it well in advance, and will leave very quietly without being seen. If you ever surprise a bobcat resting, you are certain to be greeted with a series of explosive growls and hisses as the cat makes an undignified retreat into the brush. Having long legs, it appears to bound very much like a rabbit when running.

The bobcat is most often seen at night, usually as it crosses the road ahead of your car. It often travels considerable distances, sometimes because food is scarce and sometimes apparently just because it is restless. Males are especially active and may cover several miles in a single night. It is very curious and investigates whatever catches its attention. A jumble of fallen trees is certain to be examined very thoroughly. Items that have been discarded along the trails, such as candy wrappers and bits of paper, demand inspection. Occasionally it stops and sharpens its claws on a convenient tree, much like a domestic cat. These marks may sometimes be observed by the sharp-eyed hiker.

The bobcat's hunting technique is simple. The hunting area is covered very thoroughly. It wanders back and forth, crossing and recrossing its own trail, checking all the time to be sure it hasn't missed something that can be eaten. In this way, it is almost certain to find the runways of any mice or the burrows of any other rodents in the area. It requires a fairly large territory to supply it with all the food it needs. If food is abundant, a territory of about five square miles may be sufficient; much more if food is scarce. Its hunting success is dependent upon the element of surprise, and it catches large numbers of small rodents, especially mice, shrews, and woodrats. Chipmunks, ground squirrels, marmots, cottontails, and tree squirrels are also important prey. It has been known to kill a deer if one is found in deep snow where it cannot run. It also kills an occasional careless fawn. Quail and dusky grouse are caught whenever the opportunity arises. It eats insects, and will even accept carrion if the meat isn't too spoiled. In spring, it occasionally eats fresh grass and tender leaves. Like some of the other large predators, it

will attack a porcupine, enduring the pain and discomfort of the sharp quills it is certain to receive.

Winter is normally mating time, although bobcats may mate at any time during the year. Listening to the noises made by mating activities as they take place on a moonlit night is something you will never forget. The female sits crouched low to the ground, while the male walks around her. All the while both indulge in blood-curdling screams and yowls, not unlike alley cats. This goes on for some time before the female accepts the male. After the mating, he goes on his way. About seven weeks later, the kittens are born. The mother prepares for their arrival by finding a well-hidden rock ledge, or hollow log or stump. Usually there are two or three young, although there are sometimes four. The new-born kittens are well furred, but unable to see. Nine days later the eyes open. Weaning takes place a few days later, and their diet changes from milk to meat. Once the kittens are large enough to handle themselves effectively, they are trained in hunting skills. Their training continues until fall. The young bobcats may stay together through their first winter, while their mother lives alone.

The bobcat in the wilds has few enemies. An adult can put up a fierce fight, and no animal in the Sierra deliberately attacks this hissing, spitting, growling mass of fury. Man and disease are its worst enemies. Fortunately, the place of the bobcat in the Sierran ecology is becoming recognized, and it is now being given more protection than was formerly the case.

OCCURRENCE AND DISTRIBUTION:

Sequoia–Kings Canyon: Common generally. Foothill Zone into High Sierra Zone.

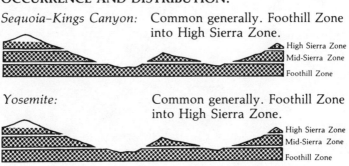

Yosemite: Common generally. Foothill Zone into High Sierra Zone.

The Insect Eaters

These animals are tiny predators, and they prey on a wide variety of insects and insect larvae. While they eat some insects beneficial to man, they also destroy large numbers of injurious ones. In addition to their insect diet, shrews may also include the flesh of small rodents, especially mice. All the insect eaters are near the bottom of the food chain and are themselves food for larger predators.

Shrews
Sorex spp.

The shrew might be described as the smallest and most destructive bundle of fury in the forest; an incredible appetite on the prowl; and, ounce for ounce the best and most courageous fighter in the Sierra. This should make it one of our best known and most frequently studied animals, but such is not the case. The very nature of the shrew and how it lives makes detailed studies very difficult.

Seeing it darting from one bit of ground cover to another, you might mistake it for a small mouse. Tail and all, it measures only about three inches long, but every inch is concentrated energy. Except when it takes a few moments off to sleep or groom itself, it is constantly on the move searching for food. Paying little attention to possible danger, it scurries through the fallen leaves, searching rotting logs, and other debris for anything that can be eaten. Its movements are nervous and erratic. It travels in quick, jerky lunges, changing direction with astonishing rapidity, emitting all the while high-pitched, twittering sounds. Its eyes are very weak, but its sense of smell and hearing are strong. Its slender, sharp-pointed nose is constantly in motion as it probes every possible place where food might be found.

The shrew burns up energy at an unbelievable rate, and consumes its own weight in food about every three hours. If forced to go without food for even a few hours, it will starve. For the most part, it eats various types of animal life, and its diet is quite varied. Its primary foods include crickets, beetles of all sorts, ants, caterpillars, snails, and earthworms. Occasionally it eats salamanders and small lizards. A young mouse is a delicacy, and the shrew is not at all adverse to attacking and killing an adult mouse twice its own size. When it bites it injects a mild poison which helps to subdue its prey. If necessary, it will eat berries, but only if other food cannot be found. The constant mad search for food takes its toll, however, and the shrew has a very short life. Usually it is dead by the time it reaches an age of fourteen months, although occasionally one may live to the ripe old age of sixteen months—a plain case of burning itself out by living too fast a life!

It is active winter and summer. When it is not killing and eating other animals, it spends part of its time fighting with others of its kind. It attacks its opponent with complete abandon, punctuating the battle with high-pitched squeals. These are fierce battles, and if the tiny warrior lives out a normal life span, it will likely have lost a toe, a tail, or show numerous scars on its body. For some reason that isn't apparent, male shrews seem to be more numerous than females. This may help to account for the vicious battles between males, as such fights may be merely to drive away competition.

The home life of a shrew is limited to only a few weeks. For about the only time during his existence, the male manages to get along reasonably well with another shrew—this time his mate. He is on his good behavior during the mating season, and before the young arrive. Then he must leave. The female usually chooses a hollow stump or a fallen log to have her family. Occasionally she may choose a burrow, but seems to prefer the better protection offered by these other sites. She prepares her nest of grass, small leaves and other soft materials she can find. The number of young may vary from three to ten. When first born each baby is a tiny, pink, wrinkled creature about the size of an adult honeybee. It is naked at birth, but quickly begins to grow a fur coat. By the time it is a week old, it can crawl. When two weeks old it has a completely furred body and is rapidly developing a set of teeth. A week to ten days later, its eyes will open. It has grown at an amazing rate and is ready to be weaned. The mother does not wait long before sending the young out to care for themselves, as she soon begins to prepare for a second family. Before the summer is over, she may have a third.

The young shrew, completely untrained in the ways of the world it must face, has an uncertain future. Wherever it goes, night or day, disaster awaits it. Should it be seen by a hawk, owl, weasel, fox, bobcat, or coyote, or by a king-snake or a bullsnake, it is unlikely to escape. It must depend upon its quickness in darting from cover to cover to escape notice. A pair of scent glands that secrete a vile smelling musk help to discourage some predators.

Trying to see a shrew is a guessing game. The best bet is to choose a place where there are down branches, logs and leaves, and sit down to watch. If you have chosen the right place, the chances are good that you will eventually see a shrew as it dashes about in its search for food.

There are several kinds of shrews in the Sierra, mostly in the forested and meadow areas. Unlike its relatives, the northern water shrew lives around streams and wet areas. It can swim and walk on the bottom of a stream where it catches small fishes and other forms of aquatic life. Holding bubbles of water on the bottoms of its feet, this shrew can actually walk on water!

OCCURRENCE AND DISTRIBUTION:

Dusky Shrew *(Sorex obscurus)*

Sequoia–Kings Canyon and Yosemite: Common. High Sierra Zone.

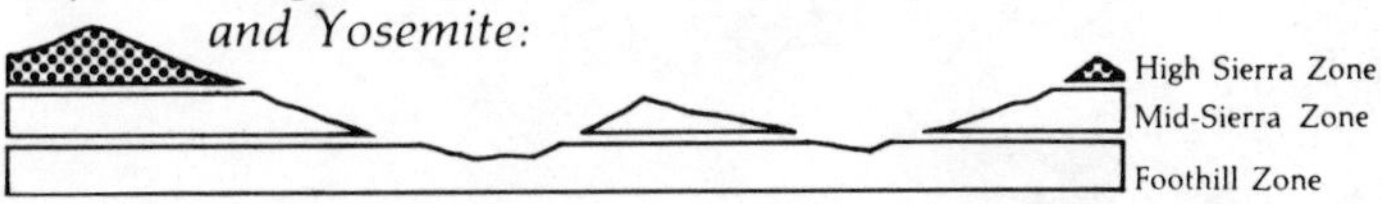

High Sierra Zone
Mid-Sierra Zone
Foothill Zone

Mt. Lyell Shrew *(Sorex lyelli)*

Sequoia–Kings Canyon: Not reported.

Yosemite: Rare. Mid-Sierra Zone and High Sierra Zone in vicinity of Mt. Lyell.

High Sierra Zone
Mid-Sierra Zone
Foothill Zone

Northern Water Shrew *(Sorex palustris)*

Sequoia–Kings Canyon and Yosemite: Rare. High Sierra Zone.

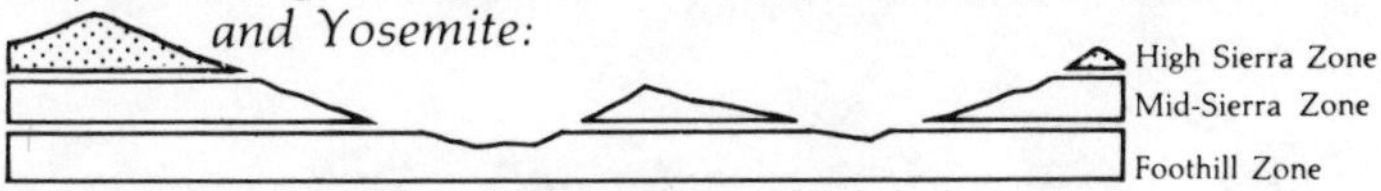

High Sierra Zone
Mid-Sierra Zone
Foothill Zone

Trowbridge Shrew *(Sorex trowbridgii)*

Sequoia–Kings Canyon and Yosemite: Common. Mid-Sierra Zone.

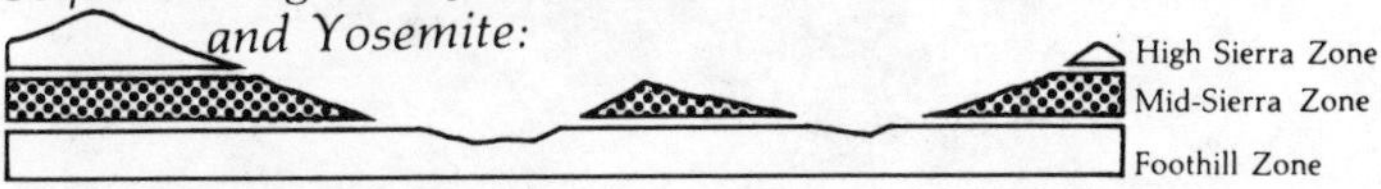

High Sierra Zone
Mid-Sierra Zone
Foothill Zone

Vagrant Shrew *(Sorex vagrans)*

Sequoia–Kings Canyon: Rare. High Sierra Zone in upper river drainages.

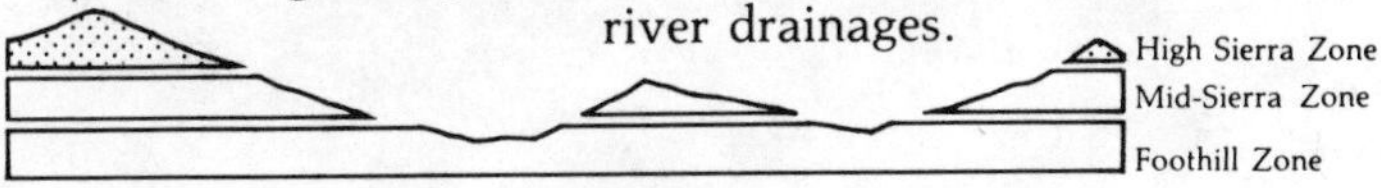

High Sierra Zone
Mid-Sierra Zone
Foothill Zone

Yosemite: Not recorded.

California
Mole

Scapanus latimanus

The chances are you may walk right over the home of this animal without knowing it, and you will probably never see a mole alive or dead. It is seldom seen above ground, and its den and workings are easily overlooked unless you know what you are seeing. The best evidence that you are in its home territory is a low, slightly arched ridge of dirt that wanders aimlessly across a meadow or opening in the forest. This ridge is the roof of one of the mole's many tunnels.

The mole spends its life underground, and is well designed to do so. It is strictly a digger, and its thick shoulders, short neck, long-snouted head and large, shovel-like front feet are ideally adapted for its only kind of activity—digging. Its fur is very soft and velvety and lies flat in any direction, allowing the animal to move smoothly forward or backward in its tunnels. It has a very short tail, enabling it to turn around in a tunnel easily. It can only distinguish light from darkness, for its eyes have degenerated to the point that they have nearly disappeared. Its ears are scarcely visible, but it is very sensitive to vibrations around it.

The composition of the soil determines where the mole will make its home. The soil depth along the ground surface must not be too loose or sandy, as the roofs of the tunnels might collapse. The tunnels are dug to enable the mole to find food, most of which is found in soils that are suitable for tunneling. The mole makes two kinds of tunnels—one deep in the ground, one near the surface. The deep tunnel leads to its bedroom, where it lives throughout the year. From the bedroom, there are normally several openings leading to the surface tunnels. Usually the bedroom is located beneath a boulder, stump or bush, giving added protection against predators.

If the surface soil is relatively soft, the mole can construct a tunnel with comparative ease. It uses its strong front feet to shovel the dirt to one side; then it forces its body forward, widening the tunnel, at the same time pushing the roof upward. In this way, a mole can dig ten to fifteen feet of tunnel per hour, even with pauses now and then to rest and eat.

Digging the deep tunnel takes much more time and labor to make, for the ground at depth is much harder. As the tunnel is dug, the mole pushes the loose material to the surface, making a "molehill" that somewhat resembles the soil mound of the pocket gopher.

The mole's food list is quite extensive. For the most part it depends upon insects, such as beetles, and insect larvae. It relishes worms of any kind, especially earthworms. Occasionally it may find seeds or flower bulbs to eat. It is active most of its waking hours, searching the soil for food, and since it must eat food equivalent to about a third of its own weight every day, it spends little time resting. Because light and darkness are of no importance to the mole, it works round the clock, but it prefers the daytime when insects and worms are more active.

The mole seems to prefer living alone, but sometimes more than one animal uses the same network of tunnels. However, this changes after mating takes place in March or early April. The mother reserves her own bedroom and others stay away. She raises only one litter a year, consisting of as many as five well-developed young. The baby mole grows rapidly, and at two months it is as large as its mother and ready to start out on its own. It is mature enough to mate the following spring.

Hunting pressure by predators is not heavy. Because the mole spends its life underground, few predators can catch it. The coyote and skunk get a few, and a snake occasionally gets into a tunnel and eats an entire family. When attacked, the mole gives off a strong, musky odor that some predators find objectionable, thus affording it some protection. Unlike most of its small rodent neighbors, the mole has a life expectancy of two years or more.

OCCURRENCE AND DISTRIBUTION:

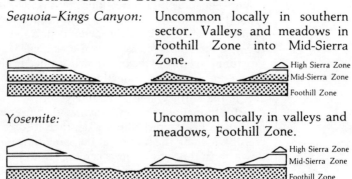

Sequoia–Kings Canyon: Uncommon locally in southern sector. Valleys and meadows in Foothill Zone into Mid-Sierra Zone.

High Sierra Zone
Mid-Sierra Zone
Foothill Zone

Yosemite: Uncommon locally in valleys and meadows, Foothill Zone.

High Sierra Zone
Mid-Sierra Zone
Foothill Zone

Bat

Suborder *Microchiroptera*

The Germans call it *der fledermaus*, the "flying mouse"; the French, *la chauve-souris*, the "bald mouse." Of course, they refer to the bat, the only flying mammal in the Sierra. However, much as it may resemble a mouse with wings, it is in no way related to one. In Mexico, bats are called *ratones voladores*, "flying rats," but bats aren't related to rats either. Actually they are rather closely related to the shrews, and the two likely evolved from a common ancestor.

The bat's wings are marvels of construction. The skin is an almost transparent membrane, so thin that newsprint can be read through it. It is delicate and easily torn. When the wings are folded the skin draws up into many crinkles, somewhat like crepe paper. Its feet are of little use except to cling tightly to its hanging place while the animal is sleeping.

It is in flight that the bat displays its most unusual abilities. Unlike birds that must maintain flying speed to stay aloft, the bat can hover, stop instantly, twist or turn in an astonishing fashion. Because its food is composed of flying insects, the ability to perform such acrobatics enables it to catch a meal with ease. Coupled with his aerial agility is his echo-location system that enables him to locate flying insects and avoid obstacles while in flight. This system operates something like sonar. The bat utters short bursts of supersonic sound waves that echo back from the insect or obstacles to its sensitive ears. The ears are large and especially designed to catch the slightest vibration. It literally "sees" by the use of sound. Don't try listening for these sounds yourself, as they are emitted at a frequency much too high for the human ear to receive. Some sounds made by the bat can be heard, however. It sometimes chatters and squeaks and may make clicking noises.

The amount of food captured on a successful hunt is extraordinary. During one night's feeding, the bat may easily eat its own weight in insects. It has a small stomach, so it eats rapidly until it is full, then quickly digests the meal and fills its stomach again. This may be repeated three or four times a night. The bat needs considerable water, more than it can get from the liquid found in the insects it eats. The problem is solved by visiting open water at a pond or lake in late evening. Here you may see a bat come in to drink, dipping low over the surface, scooping water into its mouth as it skims along. Scientists making studies of bats sometimes

stretch a fine wire just above the surface of the water. Here the echo-location system fails. The bat is unaware of the wire and hits it, tumbling into the water where it can be retrieved, examined and released.

Bats mate in late summer or early fall, and the young are born between May and July. Usually the female has one baby, but she may have as many as three. The tiny bat is born blind and naked. It grows rapidly and in two weeks is about half grown. During this time it may cling to the roof of a cave with other young bats, or it may go with its mother as she hunts, clutching her fur very tightly so as not to be jarred loose. The mother shows affection for her baby and bathes it daily with her tongue. She will also try to defend it if danger threatens.

The bat spends much of its life hanging head down in the dark in a cave, hollow tree, old building, or other place where it can hide from the sunlight. It emerges from its hiding place in late evening to hunt, but returns before the next sunrise. During the winter it selects a cave sufficiently deep to protect against the cold. Here it hibernates, normally with others of its kind. It does not awaken until spring arrives with temperatures warm enough to bring out flying insects. Species of bats that do not stay through the winter, migrate far enough south that they do not have a need to hibernate.

Bats have few enemies and are seldom caught. Owls and some hawks prey on them, but are not too successful. Most bats simply die of old age or from disease.

At least fifteen species of bats are known to occur in the Sierra. Other species may also occur but reliable records are lacking.

OCCURRENCE AND DISTRIBUTION:

California Bat (Myotis californicus)

Sequoia–Kings Canyon: Common. Foothill Zone into Mid-Sierra Zone.

High Sierra Zone
Mid-Sierra Zone
Foothill Zone

Yosemite: Common generally. Foothill Zone into Mid-Sierra Zone.

High Sierra Zone
Mid-Sierra Zone
Foothill Zone

Fringed Bat *(Myotis thysanodes)*
Sequoia–Kings Canyon: Not recorded.
Yosemite: Recorded but status uncertain. Mid-Sierra Zone.

Little Brown Bat *(Myotis lucifugus)*
Sequoia–Kings Canyon: Uncommon. *Mid-Sierra Zone into High Sierra Zone.*

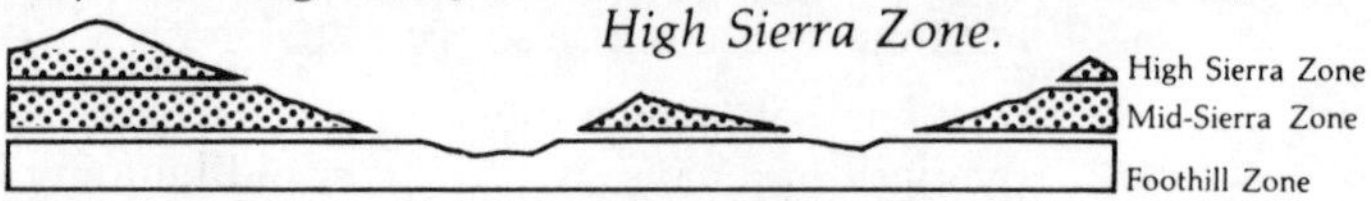

High Sierra Zone
Mid-Sierra Zone
Foothill Zone

Yosemite: Occurrence uncertain. Mid-Sierra Zone into High Sierra Zone.

Long-eared Bat *(Myotis evotis)*
Sequoia–Kings Canyon: Common. Upper Foothill Zone into Mid-Sierra Zone.

High Sierra Zone
Mid-Sierra Zone
Foothill Zone

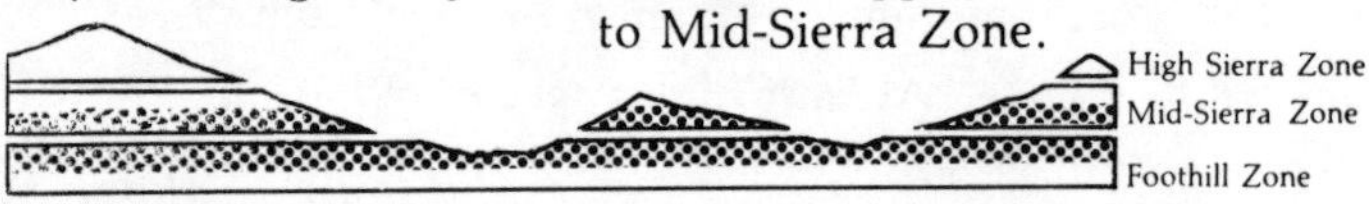

Yosemite: Occurrence uncertain. Foothill Zone into Mid-Sierra Zone.

Long-legged Bat *(Myotis volans)*
Sequoia–Kings Canyon: Rare. Recorded in southern sector, Foothill Zone into Mid-Sierra Zone.

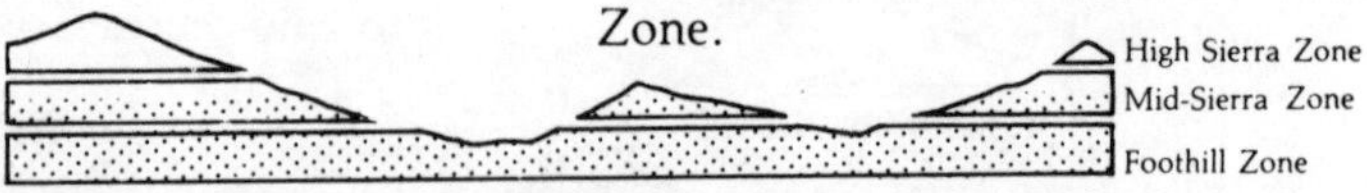

High Sierra Zone
Mid-Sierra Zone
Foothill Zone

Yosemite: Occurrence uncertain. Recorded in Mid-Sierra Zone.

Small-footed Bat *(Myotis subulatus)*

Sequoia–Kings Canyon: Not recorded.

Yosemite: Occurrence uncertain. Mid-Sierra Zone.

Yuma Bat *(Myotis yumanensis)*

Sequoia–Kings Canyon and Yosemite: Rare. Foothill Zone, southern sector.

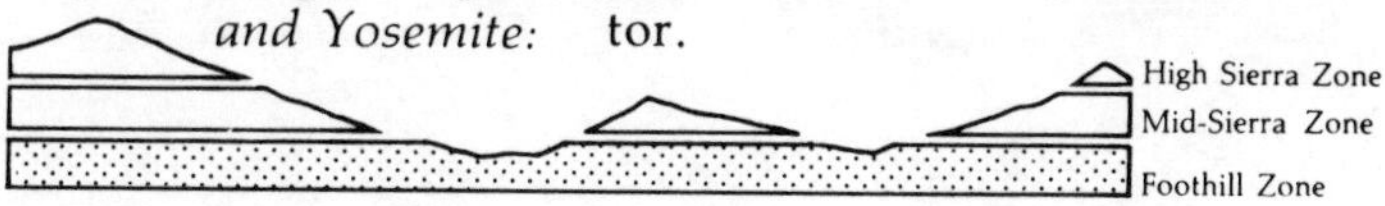

High Sierra Zone
Mid-Sierra Zone
Foothill Zone

Big Brown Bat *(Eptesicus fuscus)*

Sequoia–Kings Canyon and Yosemite: Uncommon. Mid-Sierra Zone into High Sierra Zone.

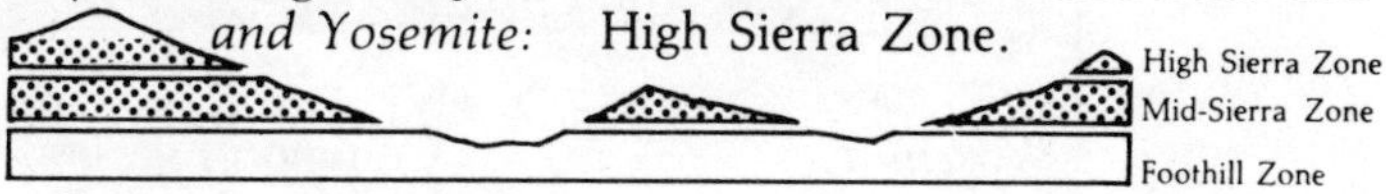

High Sierra Zone
Mid-Sierra Zone
Foothill Zone

Big-eared Bat *(Plecotus townsendii)*

Sequoia–Kings Canyon: Recorded from southern sector, but occurrence uncertain regarding range.

Yosemite: Not recorded.

Hoary Bat *(Lasiurus cinereus)*

Sequoia–Kings Canyon: Not recorded.

Yosemite: Occurrence uncertain. Mid-Sierra Zone.

Mastiff Bat *(Eumops perotas)*

Sequoia–Kings Canyon: Not recorded.

Yosemite: Occurrence uncertain. Mid-Sierra Zone.

Mexican Free-tailed Bat *(Tadarida brasiliensis)*

Sequoia–Kings Canyon: Abundant locally in southern sector, Foothill Zone into Mid-Sierra Zone. Not recorded in north but believed to be present.

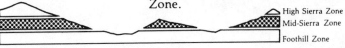

High Sierra Zone
Mid-Sierra Zone
Foothill Zone

Yosemite: Common generally. Mid-Sierra Zone.

High Sierra Zone
Mid-Sierra Zone
Foothill Zone

Pallid Bat *(Antrozous pallidus)*

Sequoia–Kings Canyon: Rare. Mid-Sierra Zone.

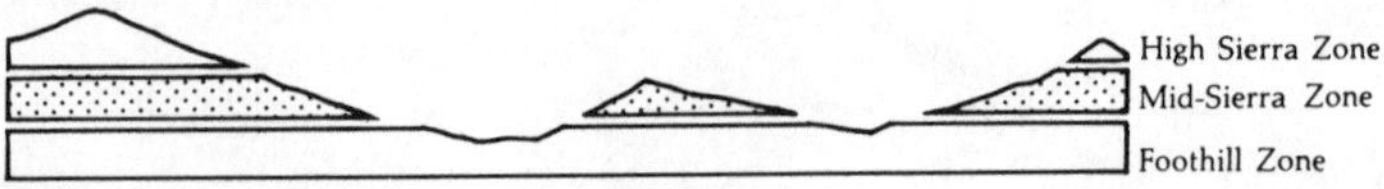

High Sierra Zone
Mid-Sierra Zone
Foothill Zone

Yosemite: Occurrence uncertain. Mid-Sierra Zone.

Spotted Bat *(Euderma maculata)*

Sequoia–Kings Canyon: Not recorded.

Yosemite: Rare. Only two records for
                            park. Mid-Sierra Zone.

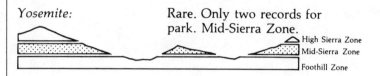

Western Pipistrelle *(Pipistrellus hesperus)*

Sequoia–Kings Canyon: Common   in   southern   sector,
                          Foothill Zone into Mid-Sierra
                          Zone. Not recorded in northern
                          sector but undoubtedly present.

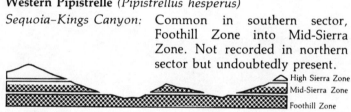

Yosemite: Common   generally.   Mid-Sierra
                           Zone.

The Introduced Species

Various kinds of mammals have been introduced into the parks, some by design and some by chance. Most of these animals failed to adapt to the Sierra environment, and soon disappeared. Only three species, the roof rat, the house mouse, and the opossum have ever succeeded in adapting. Of these, only the opossum has a wide distribution and is of any real significance in the wildlife scene. No records have been obtained of the roof rat or the house mouse for many years, and they may now have disappeared from all three parks. Hopefully this is so.

Opossum
Didelphis marsupialis

The opossum is not the only mammal in the Sierra that carries its babies along when traveling, but it is the only one that carries them in a pouch. Even more unusual, the babies enter the pouch before they can see, and their mother doesn't put them there!

The raising of an opossum family is a truly unusual event. The female normally breeds during the late winter or early spring. She prepares for the arrival of her family by selecting a cavity in a tree, hollow log or a burrow, often one deserted by some other animal. She makes a nest of grasses, lining it well to keep out the winter cold. Then she awaits the birth of her young.

The young are born prematurely, thirteen days after breeding. Each baby has a body wall that is almost transparent, and the internal organs are visible through its thin skin. The young opossum is unbelievably tiny, weighing around one-tenth to one-fifteenth of an ounce, and no larger than a small bumblebee. The entire litter could fit comfortably inside a large serving spoon. The baby's eyes and ears have not developed, and its legs are formless stumps. No sooner is it born than it begins the crucial task of trying to reach one of the mother's teats. Pulling itself along by its tiny front feet, moving purely by instinct, it works its way over the coarse hair and fur on the stomach to the small opening into the mother's pouch. It is vital that this can be done quickly, as it can easily become chilled and not survive. Finding the pouch opening, it pulls itself inside and searches for one of the life-giving teats. When one is found, it attaches itself very firmly and begins to nurse. There are twelve teats inside the pouch, but there may be as many as eighteen babies born at one time. Thus the first twelve to find the pouch survive, while the latecomers die. At no time does the mother help her babies in any way.

During its first week, the weight of the new-born baby increases about ten times. By the time two months have passed, it is as large as a mouse. Living as it does in the pouch, it goes wherever the mother goes, but now it frequently views the world from outside the pouch, riding on her back. By the end of the third month, it can take care of itself, and the mother sends it out to find its place in the world. Its first problem is to find a new home. Being a poor digger, it frequently takes over an old burrow and does some remodeling; or it may move into a deserted squirrel nest in a tree top. If all else fails, it may even move into a burrow already occupied by a skunk family who will usually tolerate their new tenant.

Food is seldom a problem for the opossum eats almost anything. It prefers meat and feeds on mice, lizards, frogs, and small snakes. It will also eat mushrooms, wild grapes, other fruits, eggs, and insects. Usually it can find a good supply of these items on only a few acres of land; thus its hunting territory is not large. It is an expert climber, and uses its prehensile tail to anchor itself as it moves along the branches searching for birds or eggs. It often hunts along the banks of streams.

The opossum is a poor fighter in spite of having an array of sharp teeth. However, if it fails to intimidate the enemy it quickly resorts to "playing dead." Falling to the ground, it becomes limp, closes its eyes, and, to all appearances, has died. Sometimes this bit of acting is successful and the enemy leaves it alone. Some wily opossums have been known to live for as much as seven years. However, some enemies aren't fooled, and the "dead" opossum becomes a hearty meal for a bobcat, coyote, fox or horned owl.

The opossum is not native to the West, and its impact upon the ecology of the Sierra has not yet been determined. It has provided an additional source of easy-to-get food for the larger predators. This to some extent lessens the hunting pressures on a number of native species. However, it competes with several of these animals for the available food. One thing is certain, the opossum is a hardy species and is now well established over much of the state. It will undoubtedly play an important role in the future of the park wildlife.

The opossum was introduced into California between 1905 and 1910. By 1924 it was recorded from the western foothills of Sequoia. Since that time it has been found in Yosemite Valley, and several have been seen at Grant Grove in Kings Canyon National Park.

OCCURRENCE AND DISTRIBUTION:

Sequoia–Kings Canyon: Common locally. Foothill Zone into lower Mid-Sierra Zone.

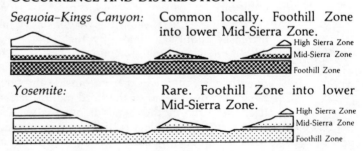

Yosemite: Rare. Foothill Zone into lower Mid-Sierra Zone.